Mediterranean Diet Cookbook for Beginners

*150 Easy, Tasty & Nutritious Recipes
for a Healthy Lifestyle
No - Stress 4 Weeks Meal Plan
and Shopping List Included*

Table of Contents

Introduction

A Mediterranean Diet Cookbook is your gateway to exploring one of the world's healthiest and most flavorful diets. It offers a collection of vibrant recipes that capture the essence of Mediterranean cuisine. This cookbook emphasizes consuming plant-based foods, healthy fats, and lean proteins, which benefit weight management and overall health.

What You'll Find Inside:

Diverse Recipes: From simple salads and hearty soups to luxurious seafood dishes and aromatic stews, the recipes are designed to be accessible, making it easy for anyone to bring the tastes of the Mediterranean into their kitchen.

Nutritional Insights: Each recipe includes detailed nutritional information, helping you align with the diet's benefits, such as improved heart health and longevity.

Practical Tips: The cookbook includes tips for meal planning and ingredient substitutions, catering to various dietary needs and preferences, and ensuring flexibility in maintaining a Mediterranean diet.

Ideal for Beginners and Seasoned Cooks:

Whether new to the Mediterranean diet or looking to expand your recipe collection, this cookbook offers a comprehensive and engaging approach to healthful eating that emphasizes flavor, variety, and enjoyment.

By adopting the recipes and principles outlined in a Mediterranean Diet Cookbook, you're not just feeding your body nutritious meals—you're embracing a wholesome way of life that celebrates food as a source of pleasure, health, and community.

Chapter 1
Basics of the Mediterranean Diet

The Essence of the Mediterranean Diet

The Mediterranean diet is more than just a meal plan; it's a lifestyle embraced by people from the Mediterranean region, including countries like Italy, Spain, and Greece. Renowned for its health benefits and delicious flavors, this diet has gained popularity worldwide for its balanced approach to eating.

Origins and Core Components

The Mediterranean diet is rooted in the Mediterranean basin's traditional dietary patterns in the early 1960s. People in this region had lower rates of chronic diseases and higher life expectancy than other parts of the world, primarily attributed to their diet and lifestyle.

The core components of the Mediterranean diet include:

Abundant Plant Foods: *Fruits, vegetables, whole grains, nuts, and seeds form the foundation of the diet. These foods are high in fiber, vitamins, and minerals and are consumed in large quantities daily.*

Healthy Fats: *Olive oil is the principal source of fat, replacing other oils and fats like butter. It's used for cooking, dressings, and even as a table condiment. Olive oil provides monounsaturated fat, which is beneficial for heart health.*

Moderate Fish and Poultry: *Fish and seafood are eaten regularly, providing a good source of omega-3 fatty acids. Poultry is consumed in moderate amounts, while red meat is eaten sparingly.*

Dairy in Moderation: *Dairy products, especially cheese and yogurt, are consumed moderately. These provide calcium and protein.*

Limited Red Meat and Sweets: *Red meat is limited to a few times a month, and sweets are consumed rarely, usually on special occasions.*

Wine in Moderation: *Wine is generally consumed moderately, generally with meals. When consumed responsibly, it's believed to contribute to heart health.*

Lifestyle Factors

The diet also emphasizes the importance of how and with whom you eat. Meals are often seen as a social event to be enjoyed with family and friends, contributing to the diet's mental health benefits. Physical activity, such as walking and gardening, plays an integral part in this lifestyle, balancing calorie intake with energy expenditure.

Sustainability

Another significant advantage of the Mediterranean diet is its focus on seasonal and local foods, making it environmentally sustainable. It promotes the consumption of products from local producers and farmers, which supports the local economy and reduces the carbon footprint associated with long-distance food transport.

Health Benefits of the Mediterranean Lifestyle

The Mediterranean lifestyle, encompassing a diet and a way of life practiced by people from countries surrounding the Mediterranean Sea, is often lauded for its numerous health benefits. Here's a detailed look at what makes this lifestyle so beneficial.

1. Heart Health

The Mediterranean diet is famed for its cardiovascular benefits. Rich in olive oil, fruits, vegetables, nuts, and fish, it provides a good balance of healthy fats and high-fiber foods that can help reduce cholesterol levels and lower the risk of heart disease.

2. Weight Management

Although not designed as a weight-loss plan, the Mediterranean diet can lead to weight loss and help maintain a healthy weight. Its emphasis on whole foods and healthy fats helps promote a feeling of fullness and reduces the likelihood of overeating.

3. Diabetes Prevention and Control

The Mediterranean lifestyle may help prevent type 2 diabetes. The diet's high fiber content helps slow digestion and prevent blood sugar spikes, while healthy fats can improve insulin sensitivity.

4. Cancer Prevention

Research suggests that the Mediterranean diet's antioxidant and anti-inflammatory properties could lower the risk of various types of cancer, including breast and colorectal cancer. The diet's emphasis on fruits, vegetables, and whole grains, all rich in antioxidants, plays a crucial role in cancer prevention.

5. Brain Health

There's evidence that the Mediterranean diet can improve brain function and reduce the risk of neurodegenerative diseases like Alzheimer's. The diet's nutrients, such as omega-3 fatty acids, antioxidants, and vitamins, are essential for brain health.

6. Bone Health

The intake of olive oil and leafy greens, which are high in calcium and vitamin D, benefit bone health. These nutrients are vital in reducing the risk of osteoporosis and fractures in older people.

7. Longevity

Following a Mediterranean diet can also increase longevity. The diet's focus on whole, nutrient-rich foods can improve overall health, potentially leading to a longer life.

8. Mental Health

There is growing evidence linking diet and mental health, particularly depression and anxiety. The Mediterranean diet's rich intake of nutrients has been associated with lower levels of depression and better mental well-being.

9. Social Benefits

The Mediterranean lifestyle also emphasizes social interactions during mealtimes, which can improve mental health and enhance life satisfaction. Sharing meals can reduce isolation and increase feelings of community and happiness.

What to Eat and Avoid

Foods to Eat on the Mediterranean Diet

1. Fruits and Vegetables

Why: Fruits and vegetables are the cornerstones of the Mediterranean diet, and they are high in vitamins, minerals, fiber, and antioxidants.

Benefits: They help reduce disease risk and provide essential nutrients for overall health.

Tips: Choose a variety of colors and types. Incorporate vegetables into every meal and enjoy fruit as a daily dessert or snack.

2. Whole Grains

Why: Whole grains are minimally processed and retain fiber and nutrients.

Benefits: They provide sustained energy and help maintain healthy digestion and cholesterol levels.

Tips: Choose whole-grain bread, pasta, and cereals. Experiment with grains like farro, quinoa, and bulgur in salads and sides.

3. Healthy Fats

Why: Unsaturated fats derived primarily from olive oil, nuts, and seeds benefit heart health.

Benefits: They help absorb vitamins and reduce the risk of heart disease.

Tips: Use olive oil for cooking and dressing. Include a handful of nuts or seeds as a snack or in salads.

4. Legumes

Why: Legumes are excellent protein sources and rich in fiber.

Benefits: They support heart health and help maintain stable blood sugar levels.

Tips: Incorporate lentils, beans, and chickpeas into soups, salads, and stews.

5. Fish and Seafood

Why: High omega-3 fatty acids are crucial for heart and brain health.

Benefits: Regular consumption can decrease inflammation and improve cardiovascular health.

Tips: Aim for at least two servings per week. Grill, bake, or broil fish to retain its nutritional value.

6. Herbs and Spices

Why: They add flavors without extra salt or fat.

Benefits: Many herbs and spices offer anti-inflammatory and antioxidant properties.

Tips: Experiment with garlic, basil, mint, rosemary, and turmeric.

Foods to Limit or Avoid

1. Red Meat

Why: High in saturated fats, contributing to heart disease.

Tips: Limit red meat a few times monthly and opt for lean cuts.

2. Refined Grains and Sugars

Why: These offer little nutritional value and contribute to weight gain and diabetes.

Tips: Avoid white bread, pasta, and sugary desserts. Choose whole-grain alternatives.

3. Processed Foods

Why: Often high in unhealthy fats, salt, and calories.

Tips: Read labels carefully and choose items with short, recognizable ingredient lists.

4. High-fat Dairy Products

Why: Like red meat, high-fat dairy products can be rich in unhealthy saturated fats.

Tips: Opt for low-fat or plant-based alternatives.

Reading Food Labels

To adhere to the Mediterranean diet, understanding food labels is crucial.

Look for:

Low Sodium: Aim for less than 5% of the daily value per serving.

Whole Grains: The first ingredient should be whole grain.

Sugars: Avoid foods with added sugars near the top of the ingredient list.

Adopting the Mediterranean diet can be a delightful and healthful journey. It's not just about restricting certain foods but enjoying various nutritious options that promote a healthier life. Experiment with new recipes and flavors to fully embrace Mediterranean eating. Your body and taste buds will thank you for the vibrant variety and the wholesome benefits.

Chapter 2
Breakfast

Greek Yogurt Parfait with Honey and Walnuts

INGREDIENTS

- Greek Yogurt: 2 cups
- Honey: 4 tablespoons
- Walnuts: 1/2 cup, chopped
- Fresh Berries: 1 cup (optional)
- Granola: 1/2 cup (optional)
- Cinnamon: 1/2 teaspoon (optional)
- Mint Leaves: For garnish

 Prep Time: 10 min

 Cook Time: 5 min

 Serves: 4

Nutritional Info (per serving):

Calories: 280/Protein: 10g/Carbs: 25g/Fats: 16g/Fiber: 2g/Sodium: 50mg

DIRECTIONS

Toast chopped walnuts in a skillet for 3-5 minutes.
Combine yogurt with one tablespoon of honey and cinnamon (if using).
Layer yogurt, berries, walnuts, and granola in 4 glasses. Drizzle with remaining honey.
Garnish with mint leaves and serve immediately or refrigerate.

Mediterranean Frittata with Spinach and Feta

INGREDIENTS

- Eggs: 6 large
- Spinach: 2 cups, chopped
- Feta Cheese: 1/2 cup, crumbled
- Red Onion: 1 small, chopped
- Cherry Tomatoes: 1/2 cup, halved
- Olive Oil: 1 tablespoon
- Garlic: 2 cloves, minced
- Dried Oregano: 1 teaspoon
- Salt and Pepper: To taste
- Fresh Parsley/Basil (optional): 2 tablespoons, chopped

 Prep Time: 10 min

 Cook Time: 20 min

 Serves: 4

Nutritional Info (per serving):

Calories: 200/Protein: 12g/Carbs: 5g/Fats: 15g/Fiber: 1g/Sodium: 400mg

DIRECTIONS

Preheat to 375°F (190°C).
Heat olive oil in an oven-safe skillet. Sauté onion and garlic for 3-4 minutes. Add spinach and cook until wilted. Season with salt, pepper, and oregano.
Whisk eggs, then stir in feta and tomatoes. Pour the mixture over the veggies into the skillet. Cook on the stovetop for 2-3 minutes until the edges are set.
Transfer the skillet to the oven, and bake for 10-12 minutes until set.
Garnish with parsley or basil, slice, and serve warm.

Olive and Tomato Breakfast Bruschetta

INGREDIENTS

- Whole Grain Bread: 4 slices
- Olive Oil: 2 tablespoons
- Garlic: 1 clove, halved
- Cherry Tomatoes: 1 cup, halved
- Kalamata Olives: 1/2 cup, chopped
- Fresh Basil: 1/4 cup, chopped
- Feta Cheese: 1/4 cup, crumbled (optional)
- Salt and Pepper: To taste
- Balsamic Glaze: 1 tablespoon (optional)

 Prep Time: 10 min

 Cook Time: 5 min

 Serves: 4

Nutritional Info (per serving):

Calories: 180/Protein: 4g/Carbs: 20g/Fats: 10g/Fiber: 3g/Sodium: 300mg

DIRECTIONS

Brush bread with olive oil and toast in a skillet for 2-3 minutes per side. Rub with garlic.
Mix tomatoes, olives, basil, salt, and pepper.
Top the bread with a tomato mixture, and add feta and balsamic glaze if desired.
Serve immediately.

Cucumber and Herb Labneh on Toast

INGREDIENTS

- Whole Grain Bread: 4 slices
- Labneh: 1 cup
- Cucumber: 1 medium, thinly sliced
- Fresh Mint: 2 tbsp, chopped
- Fresh Dill: 2 tbsp, chopped
- Olive Oil: 1 tbsp
- Lemon Zest: 1 tsp
- Salt and Pepper: To taste
- Sumac: 1/2 tsp (optional)

 Prep Time: 10 min

 Cook Time: 5 min

 Serves: 4

Nutritional Info (per serving):

Calories: 200/Protein: 6g/Carbs: 20g/Fats: 10g/Fiber: 3g/Sodium: 250mg

DIRECTIONS

Toast bread slices until golden.
Mix labneh with mint, dill, lemon zest, salt, and pepper.
Spread labneh on toasted bread. Top with cucumber slices.
Drizzle with olive oil and sprinkle with sumac. Serve immediately.

Spinach and Ricotta Breakfast Pitas

INGREDIENTS

- Whole Wheat Pitas: 4
- Fresh Spinach: 4 cups, chopped
- Ricotta Cheese: 1 cup
- Olive Oil: 1 tbsp
- Garlic: 2 cloves, minced
- Red Onion: 1 small, chopped
- Eggs: 2 large, beaten
- Feta Cheese: 1/4 cup, crumbled (optional)
- Fresh Dill/Parsley: 2 tbsp, chopped (optional)
- Salt and Pepper: To taste
- Lemon Wedges: For serving (optional)

 Prep Time: 10 min

 Cook Time: 10 min

 Serves: 4

Nutritional Info (per serving):

Calories: 280/Protein: 12g/Carbs: 30g/Fats: 12g/Fiber: 5g/Sodium: 450mg

DIRECTIONS

Heat olive oil, sauté garlic and onion for 2-3 minutes, add spinach and cook until wilted.

Reduce heat, add beaten eggs to spinach mixture, and stir until set. Season with salt and pepper.

Spread ricotta inside pitas and fill with spinach and egg mixture. Top with feta and herbs if desired.

Serve immediately with lemon wedges.

Mediterranean Egg White Scramble

INGREDIENTS

- Egg Whites: 12 (about 1 1/2 cups)
- Olive Oil: 1 tbsp
- Red Onion: 1 small, chopped
- Bell Pepper: 1 medium, chopped
- Cherry Tomatoes: 1 cup, halved
- Fresh Spinach: 2 cups
- Feta Cheese: 1/4 cup, crumbled (optional)
- Fresh Basil/Parsley: 2 tbsp, chopped (optional)
- Salt and Pepper: To taste
- Garlic Powder: 1/2 tsp (optional)

  Prep Time: 10 min

 Cook Time: 10 min

 Serves: 4

Nutritional Info (per serving):

Calories: 120/Protein: 15g/Carbs: 6g/Fats: 5g/Fiber: 2g/Sodium: 300mg

DIRECTIONS

Heat olive oil, and sauté onion and bell pepper for 3-4 minutes. Add tomatoes and cook for 2 minutes, then add spinach and cook until wilted.

Pour the egg whites into the skillet and season with salt, pepper, and garlic powder. Stir gently and cook until the egg whites are set, about 3-4 minutes.

Remove from heat, sprinkle with crumbled feta and fresh herbs if using. Serve immediately.

Quinoa and Chia Porridge with Apricots

INGREDIENTS

- Quinoa: 1 cup, rinsed
- Chia Seeds: 2 tbsp
- Water: 2 cups
- Almond Milk: 1 cup (unsweetened)
- Dried Apricots: 1/2 cup, chopped
- Honey: 2 tbsp (optional)
- Ground Cinnamon: 1/2 tsp
- Vanilla Extract: 1 tsp
- Slivered Almonds: 1/4 cup (optional)
- Fresh Berries: 1/2 cup (optional)

 Prep Time: 5 min

 Cook Time: 20 min

 Serves: 4

Nutritional Info (per serving):

Calories: 220/Protein: 6g/Carbs: 36g/Fats: 6g/Fiber: 6g/Sodium: 20mg

DIRECTIONS

Combine quinoa and water in a saucepan. Bring to a boil, then simmer for 15 minutes until tender.

Stir in almond milk, chia seeds, apricots, honey, cinnamon, and vanilla. Simmer for 5 minutes until thickened.

Divide into bowls and top with almonds and berries if desired.

Almond and Fig Breakfast Bars

INGREDIENTS

- Rolled Oats: 1 cup
- Almond Flour: 1/2 cup
- Dried Figs: 1/2 cup, chopped
- Almonds: 1/4 cup, chopped
- Honey: 1/4 cup
- Almond Butter: 1/4 cup
- Chia Seeds: 2 tbsp
- Ground Cinnamon: 1/2 tsp
- Vanilla Extract: 1 tsp
- Salt: A pinch

 Prep Time: 10 min

 Cook Time: 20 min

 Serves: 4 (8 bars)

Nutritional Info (per serving):

Calories: 250/Protein: 6g/Carbs:32g/Fats: 12g/Fiber: 5g/Sodium: 50mg

DIRECTIONS

Preheat to 350°F (175°C). Line an 8x8-inch baking pan with parchment paper.

Combine oats, almond flour, figs, almonds, chia seeds, cinnamon, and salt.

Heat honey and almond butter in a saucepan until smooth. Stir in vanilla.

Mix wet and dry ingredients. Press into the pan and bake for 15-20 minutes. Cool before cutting.

Cut into bars and enjoy.

Za'atar Seasoned Avocado Toast

INGREDIENTS

- Whole Grain Bread: 4 slices
- Avocados: 2 ripe, mashed
- Lemon Juice: 1 tbsp
- Za'atar: 2 tsp
- Olive Oil: 1 tbsp
- Salt and Pepper: To taste
- Cherry Tomatoes: 1/2 cup, halved (optional)
- Feta Cheese: 1/4 cup, crumbled (optional)
- Fresh Herbs: 2 tbsp, chopped (optional)

 Prep Time: 10 min   Cook Time: 5 min   Serves: 4

Nutritional Info (per serving):

Calories: 280/Protein: 5g/Carbs: 26g/Fats: 19g/Fiber: 8g/Sodium: 220mg

DIRECTIONS

Toast the bread until golden.

Mash avocados with lemon juice, salt, and pepper.

Spread avocado on toast and sprinkle with za'atar. Add optional toppings like tomatoes, feta, and herbs. Drizzle with olive oil.

Serve immediately for a healthy, flavorful breakfast or snack.

Smoked Salmon and Cream Cheese Crepes

INGREDIENTS

For the Crepes:

- Whole Wheat Flour: 1 cup
- Eggs: 2 large
- Milk: 1 cup
- Water: 1/2 cup
- Olive Oil: 1 tbsp
- Salt: A pinch

For the Filling:

- Smoked Salmon: 8 oz, thinly sliced
- Cream Cheese: 1/2 cup
- Lemon Juice: 1 tbsp
- Fresh Dill: 2 tbsp, chopped
- Capers: 2 tbsp
- Red Onion: 1 small, thinly sliced (optional)
- Salt and Pepper: To taste

 Prep Time: 15 min   Cook Time: 20 min   Serves: 4

Nutritional Info (per serving):

Calories: 350/Protein: 18g/Carbs:30g/Fats: 18g/Fiber: 3g/Sodium: 750mg

DIRECTIONS

Whisk flour, eggs, milk, water, olive oil, and salt until smooth. Let rest for 5 minutes. Cook in a non-stick skillet over medium heat, 1-2 minutes per side.

Mix cream cheese, lemon juice, dill, salt, and pepper.

Spread cream cheese mixture on each crepe. Top with smoked salmon, capers, and onion. Fold or roll up.

Garnish with dill and serve immediately.

Artichoke and Roasted Pepper Omelet

INGREDIENTS

- Eggs: 8 large
- Artichoke Hearts: 1 cup, chopped
- Roasted Red Peppers: 1/2 cup, chopped
- Olive Oil: 2 tbsp
- Red Onion: 1 small, chopped
- Garlic: 2 cloves, minced
- Feta Cheese: 1/4 cup, crumbled (optional)
- Fresh Parsley: 2 tbsp, chopped
- Salt and Pepper: To taste
- Fresh Basil/Oregano: 1 tbsp, chopped (optional)

 Prep Time: 10 min

 Cook Time: 15 min

 Serves: 4

Nutritional Info (per serving):

Calories: 250/Protein: 14g/Carbs: 8g/Fats: 18g/Fiber: 3g/Sodium: 350mg

DIRECTIONS

Heat 1 tbsp olive oil in a skillet. Sauté onion and garlic for 2-3 minutes. Add artichokes and peppers, and cook 2-3 minutes. Set aside.
Whisk eggs with salt and pepper.
Heat the remaining olive oil in a skillet, and pour in the eggs. Once the eggs start to set, add the vegetables and feta on one side. Fold the omelet and cook until set.
Garnish with parsley and herbs. Cut into four portions and serve.

Savory Muffin with Olives and Sundried Tomatoes

INGREDIENTS

- Whole Wheat Flour: 1 cup
- Almond Flour: 1/2 cup
- Baking Powder: 1 1/2 tsp
- Eggs: 2 large
- Olive Oil: 1/4 cup
- Greek Yogurt: 1/2 cup
- Milk: 1/4 cup
- Kalamata Olives: 1/4 cup, chopped
- Sundried Tomatoes: 1/4 cup, chopped
- Feta Cheese: 1/4 cup, crumbled (optional)
- Fresh Herbs: 2 tbsp, chopped
- Salt: 1/2 tsp
- Black Pepper: 1/4 tsp

 Prep Time: 15 min

 Cook Time: 20 min

 Serves: 4 (8 muffins)

Nutritional Info (per serving):

Calories: 200/Protein: 6g/Carbs:16g/Fats: 13g/Fiber: 3g/Sodium: 300mg

DIRECTIONS

Preheat to 350°F (175°C). Line a muffin tin. Combine dry ingredients in one bowl. Whisk wet ingredients in another. Mix, then fold in olives, sundried tomatoes, feta, and herbs.
Divide batter into muffin cups. Bake for 18-20 minutes until a toothpick comes out clean.
Cool and serve warm or at room temperature.

Poached Eggs over Garlic Spinach and Toast

INGREDIENTS

- Eggs: 4 large
- Whole Grain Bread: 4 slices
- Fresh Spinach: 4 cups
- Olive Oil: 2 tbsp
- Garlic: 2 cloves, minced
- Lemon Juice: 1 tbsp
- Salt and Pepper: To taste
- Fresh Herbs (optional): 2 tbsp, chopped

 Prep Time: 10 min

 Cook Time: 15 min

 Serves: 4

Nutritional Info (per serving):

Calories: 250/Protein: 12g/Carbs: 20g/Fats: 14g/Fiber: 4g/Sodium: 400mg

DIRECTIONS

Heat 1 tbsp olive oil in a skillet. Sauté garlic for 1 minute, then add spinach and cook until wilted. Season with salt, pepper, and lemon juice.
Toast the whole grain bread slices until golden.
Simmer water in a saucepan. Add eggs and poach for 3-4 minutes until whites are set.
Place spinach on toast, top with a poached egg, drizzle with olive oil, and sprinkle with herbs.

Warm Barley and Apple Breakfast Bowl

INGREDIENTS

- Pearled Barley: 1 cup
- Water: 2 1/2 cups
- Apples: 2 medium, chopped
- Honey: 2 tbsp
- Cinnamon: 1 tsp
- Nutmeg: 1/4 tsp
- Raisins/Cranberries: 1/4 cup (optional)
- Almonds: 1/4 cup, sliced
- Greek Yogurt: 1/2 cup (optional)
- Fresh Mint/Basil: 2 tbsp, chopped (optional)

 Prep Time: 10 min

 Cook Time: 25 min

 Serves: 4

Nutritional Info (per serving):

Calories: 250/Protein: 5g/Carbs:45g/Fats: 6g/Fiber: 8g/Sodium: 10mg

DIRECTIONS

Simmer barley in water for 20 minutes until tender.
Cook apples with honey, cinnamon, and nutmeg in a skillet for 5 minutes until soft.
Mix apples with cooked barley. Divide into bowls and top with almonds and yogurt. Garnish with herbs if desired.

Baked Pear with Honey and Pecans

INGREDIENTS

- Pears: 2 large, halved and cored
- Honey: 2 tbsp
- Pecans: 1/4 cup, chopped
- Ground Cinnamon: 1/2 tsp
- Ground Nutmeg: 1/4 tsp
- Olive Oil: 1 tsp
- Greek Yogurt: 1/2 cup (optional)

Prep Time: 10 min

Cook Time: 20 min

Serves: 4

Nutritional Info (per serving):

Calories: 180/Protein: 2g/Carbs: 26g/Fats: 9g/Fiber: 4g/Sodium: 5mg

DIRECTIONS

Preheat to 350°F (175°C).

Place pear halves in a baking dish. Drizzle with olive oil and honey, then sprinkle with cinnamon and nutmeg. Top with pecans.

Bake for 20 minutes until pears are tender.

Serve warm, with a dollop of Greek yogurt if desired.

Mediterranean Smoothie with Dates and Almonds

INGREDIENTS

- Almond Milk: 2 cups
- Greek Yogurt: 1 cup
- Bananas: 2, frozen
- Medjool Dates: 8, pitted
- Almonds: 1/4 cup, soaked
- Honey: 1 tbsp (optional)
- Ground Cinnamon: 1/2 tsp
- Vanilla Extract: 1 tsp
- Ice Cubes: 1 cup (optional)

Prep Time: 10 min

Cook Time: 0 min

Serves: 4

Nutritional Info (per serving):

Calories: 250/Protein: 8g/Carbs:38g/Fats: 9g/Fiber: 5g/Sodium: 50mg

DIRECTIONS

Combine almond milk, yogurt, bananas, dates, soaked almonds, honey, cinnamon, and vanilla in a blender. Blend until smooth.

Add ice cubes for a thicker smoothie and blend again.

Pour into glasses and serve immediately.

Feta and Dill Breakfast Scones

INGREDIENTS

- Whole Wheat Flour: 1 cup
- All-Purpose Flour: 1 cup
- Baking Powder: 1 tbsp
- Salt: 1/2 tsp
- Unsalted Butter: 1/4 cup, cold and cubed
- Feta Cheese: 1/2 cup, crumbled
- Fresh Dill: 2 tbsp, chopped
- Greek Yogurt: 1/2 cup
- Milk: 1/4 cup
- Egg: 1, beaten (optional, for egg wash)

 Prep Time: 15 min
 Cook Time: 20 min
 Serves: 4 (8 scones)

Nutritional Info (per serving):

Calories: 230/Protein: 7g/Carbs: 25g/Fats: 11g/Fiber: 3g/Sodium: 400mg

DIRECTIONS

Preheat to 400°F (200°C) and line a baking sheet.
Combine flour, baking powder, and salt.
Mix in butter until the mixture is crumbly.
Stir in feta and dill.
Mix yogurt and milk, then add to the dry ingredients. Stir until just combined.
Form the dough into a circle, cut it into eight wedges, and place it on the baking sheet. Brush with egg wash if using. Bake for 18-20 minutes until golden.
Cool slightly before serving.

Pistachio and Orange Blossom Oatmeal

INGREDIENTS

- Rolled Oats: 2 cups
- Water or Almond Milk: 4 cups
- Pistachios: 1/2 cup, chopped
- Orange Blossom Water: 1 tsp
- Honey: 2 tbsp (optional)
- Orange Zest: 1 tbsp
- Ground Cinnamon: 1/2 tsp
- Salt: A pinch

 Prep Time: 5 min
 Cook Time: 10 min
 Serves: 4

Nutritional Info (per serving):

Calories: 280/Protein: 7g/Carbs:40g/Fats: 10g/Fiber: 6g/Sodium: 60mg

DIRECTIONS

Bring water or almond milk to a boil. Add oats and salt, simmer for 5-7 minutes until creamy.
Stir in orange blossom water, honey, orange zest, and cinnamon.
Mix in chopped pistachios, reserving some for garnish.
Divide into bowls and garnish with extra pistachios and orange slices if desired.

Baked Eggs with Spinach and Tomato Sauce

INGREDIENTS

- Olive Oil: 2 tbsp
- Garlic: 2 cloves, minced
- Fresh Spinach: 4 cups
- Crushed Tomatoes: 1 cup
- Tomato Paste: 1 tbsp
- Dried Oregano: 1 tsp
- Dried Basil: 1 tsp
- Red Pepper Flakes: 1/4 tsp (optional)
- Salt and Pepper: To taste
- Eggs: 4 large
- Feta Cheese: 1/4 cup, crumbled (optional)
- Fresh Parsley/Basil: 2 tbsp, chopped (for garnish)

 Prep Time: 10 min

 Cook Time: 20 min

 Serves: 4

Nutritional Info (per serving):

Calories: 220/Protein: 12g/Carbs: 10g/Fats: 15g/Fiber: 3g/Sodium: 400mg

DIRECTIONS

Preheat to 375°F (190°C).

Sauté garlic in olive oil, add spinach, and cook until wilted. Stir in tomatoes, tomato paste, oregano, basil, and seasonings. Simmer for 5 minutes.

Make wells in the sauce, and crack an egg into each.

Bake in the oven for 10-12 minutes until egg whites are set.

Top with feta and fresh herbs. Serve with whole grain toast or pita.

Citrus and Mint Fruit Salad with Greek Yogurt

INGREDIENTS

Fruit Salad:

- Oranges: 2, segmented
- Grapefruit: 1, segmented
- Strawberries: 1 cup, sliced
- Kiwi: 2, sliced
- Fresh Mint: 2 tbsp, chopped
- Honey: 1 tbsp (optional)
- Lemon Juice: 1 tbsp

Greek Yogurt Topping:

- Greek Yogurt: 1 cup
- Honey: 1 tbsp
- Vanilla Extract: 1/2 tsp

 Prep Time: 15 min

 Cook Time: 0 min

 Serves: 4

Nutritional Info (per serving):

Calories: 150/Protein: 5g/Carbs:30g/Fats: 2g/Fiber: 5g/Sodium: 20mg

DIRECTIONS

Combine orange, grapefruit, strawberries, kiwi, mint, honey, and lemon juice in a bowl.

Mix Greek yogurt, honey, and vanilla in a small bowl.

Divide fruit salad into bowls and top with yogurt.

Chapter 3
Snacks and Appetizers

Marinated Olives with Citrus and Herbs

INGREDIENTS

- Mixed Olives: 2 cups
- Olive Oil: 1/4 cup
- Garlic: 2 cloves, sliced
- Orange Zest: 1 tbsp
- Lemon Zest: 1 tbsp
- Fresh Rosemary: 1 sprig
- Fresh Thyme: 2 sprigs
- Crushed Red Pepper Flakes: 1/4 tsp (optional)
- Orange Juice: 2 tbsp
- Lemon Juice: 1 tbsp
- Salt and Pepper: To taste

 Prep Time: 10 min

 Cook Time: 5 min (plus marinating time)

 Serves: 4

Nutritional Info (per serving):

Calories: 180/Protein: 1g/Carbs: 4g/Fats: 18g/Fiber: 2g/Sodium: 700mg

DIRECTIONS

Heat olive oil over low heat. Add garlic, zest, rosemary, thyme, and red pepper flakes. Warm for 3-4 minutes until fragrant.

Toss the warm oil mixture with olives, orange juice, lemon juice, salt, and pepper. Let sit at room temperature for 1 hour or refrigerate for 24 hours. Bring to room temperature before serving.

Caprese Skewers with Balsamic Reduction

INGREDIENTS

- Cherry Tomatoes: 1 pint
- Fresh Mozzarella Balls: 8 oz
- Fresh Basil Leaves: 1/2 cup
- Balsamic Vinegar: 1/2 cup
- Olive Oil: 1 tbsp
- Salt and Pepper: To taste
- Skewers: 8-12

 Prep Time: 10 min

 Cook Time: 15 min

 Serves: 4

Nutritional Info (per serving):

Calories: 160/Protein: 6g/Carbs:8g/Fats: 12g/Fiber: 1g/Sodium: 180mg

DIRECTIONS

Simmer balsamic vinegar over medium heat for 10-15 minutes until reduced and syrupy. Let cool.

Thread a cherry tomato, mozzarella ball, and basil leaf onto each skewer. Repeat with remaining ingredients.

Drizzle skewers with olive oil and season with salt and pepper. Drizzle with balsamic reduction and serve.

Stuffed Grape Leaves (Dolmas)

INGREDIENTS

- Grape Leaves: 20-24, rinsed and drained
- Short-Grain Rice: 1 cup, rinsed
- Olive Oil: 1/4 cup, divided
- Onion: 1 small, chopped
- Pine Nuts: 2 tbsp (optional)
- Raisins or Currants: 2 tbsp (optional)
- Fresh Parsley: 1/4 cup, chopped
- Fresh Mint: 1/4 cup, chopped
- Dried Dill: 1 tsp
- Lemon Juice: 1/4 cup
- Water or Vegetable Broth: 1 1/2 cups
- Salt and Pepper: To taste

 Prep Time: 30 min

 Cook Time: 45 min

 Serves: 4

Nutritional Info (per serving):

Calories: 180/Protein: 3g/Carbs: 22g/Fats: 9g/Fiber: 3g/Sodium: 200mg

DIRECTIONS

Sauté onion in 2 tbsp olive oil until soft. Add rice, pine nuts, raisins, parsley, mint, dill, salt, and pepper. Cook for 2-3 minutes, then add 1 cup water or broth. Simmer until rice is partially cooked, about 10 minutes. Let cool.

Place 1 tbsp filling on each grape leaf, fold sides over, and roll tightly. Arrange stuffed leaves in a pot, seam side down. Drizzle with olive oil and lemon juice, add 1/2 cup water or broth. Cover with a plate and simmer for 30-40 minutes. Serve at room temperature or chilled, garnished with lemon wedges and herbs.

Fava Bean and Mint Crostini

INGREDIENTS

- Fava Beans: 1 cup (shelled)
- Whole Grain Baguette: 1 small, sliced (8 pieces)
- Olive Oil: 2 tbsp, divided
- Garlic: 1 clove, minced
- Fresh Mint: 2 tbsp, chopped
- Lemon Juice: 1 tbsp
- Salt and Pepper: To taste
- Ricotta or Feta Cheese: 1/4 cup, crumbled (optional)
- Lemon Zest: 1 tsp (optional)

 Prep Time: 15 min

 Cook Time: 10 min

 Serves: 4

Nutritional Info (per serving):

Calories: 180/Protein: 5g/Carbs:22g/Fats: 8g/Fiber: 4g/Sodium: 150mg

DIRECTIONS

Blanch fresh fava beans, then peel. If using frozen, thaw and peel.

Sauté garlic in 1 tbsp olive oil. Add fava beans and cook for 2-3 minutes. Mix the beans with mint, lemon juice, salt, and pepper.

Preheat the oven to 375°F (190°C). Brush the baguette slices with olive oil and toast for 8-10 minutes.

Spread fava bean mixture on toast. Top with cheese and lemon zest if desired.

Spinach and Feta Phyllo Triangles

INGREDIENTS

- Phyllo Dough: 6 sheets, thawed
- Fresh Spinach: 4 cups, chopped
- Feta Cheese: 1/2 cup, crumbled
- Olive Oil: 2 tbsp, plus more for brushing
- Onion: 1 small, chopped
- Garlic: 2 cloves, minced
- Fresh Dill: 2 tbsp, chopped
- Fresh Parsley: 2 tbsp, chopped
- Egg: 1, beaten
- Salt and Pepper: To taste

 Prep Time: 20 min

 Cook Time: 20 min

 Serves: 4 (12 triangles)

Nutritional Info (per serving):

Calories: 200/Protein: 7g/Carbs: 18g/Fats: 12g/Fiber: 2g/Sodium: 400mg

DIRECTIONS

Sauté onion and garlic in 1 tbsp olive oil until soft. Add spinach and cook until wilted. Mix with feta, dill, parsley, egg, salt, and pepper. Preheat oven to 375°F (190°C). Layer 3 phyllo sheets, brushing each with olive oil. Cut into 3-inch strips. Place filling at the strip's bottom and fold into triangles. Repeat with remaining phyllo and filling.
Bake on a lined sheet for 18-20 minutes until golden.
Cool slightly and serve warm.

Garlic and Herb Baked Feta

INGREDIENTS

- Feta Cheese: 1 block (8 oz)
- Olive Oil: 2 tbsp
- Garlic: 2 cloves, sliced
- Fresh Rosemary: 1 sprig
- Fresh Thyme: 2 sprigs
- Dried Oregano: 1 tsp
- Cherry Tomatoes: 1 cup, halved (optional)
- Kalamata Olives: 1/4 cup, halved (optional)
- Crushed Red Pepper Flakes: 1/4 tsp (optional)
- Lemon Zest: 1 tsp
- Fresh Parsley: 1 tbsp, chopped (for garnish)
- Salt and Pepper: To taste
- Whole Grain Bread or Pita: For serving

 Prep Time: 10 min

 Cook Time: 15 min

 Serves: 4

Nutritional Info (per serving):

Calories: 200/Protein: 7g/Carbs:4g/Fats: 18g/Fiber: 1g/Sodium: 450mg

DIRECTIONS

Preheat to 375°F (190°C).
Place feta in an ovenproof dish. Drizzle with olive oil, top with garlic, herbs, and seasonings, and add tomatoes and olives, if using.
Bake for 15 minutes until the feta is soft and golden.
Garnish with parsley and serve warm with bread or pita.

Lemon and Thyme Marinated Artichokes

INGREDIENTS

- Artichoke Hearts: 1 can (14 oz), drained and quartered
- Olive Oil: 1/4 cup
- Lemon Juice: 2 tbsp
- Lemon Zest: 1 tsp
- Fresh Thyme: 1 tbsp, chopped
- Garlic: 2 cloves, minced
- Red Pepper Flakes: 1/4 tsp (optional)
- Salt and Pepper: To taste
- Fresh Parsley: 2 tbsp, chopped (for garnish)

 Prep Time: 15 min

 Cook Time: 1-2 hours

 Serves: 4

Nutritional Info (per serving):

Calories: 120/Protein: 2g/Carbs: 8g/Fats: 10g/Fiber: 5g/Sodium: 200mg

DIRECTIONS

- Whisk together olive oil, lemon juice, zest, thyme, garlic, red pepper flakes, salt, and pepper.
Coat artichoke hearts in the marinade. Refrigerate for 1-2 hours.
Bring to room temperature, garnish with parsley, and serve.

Prosciutto-Wrapped Melon with Basil

INGREDIENTS

- Cantaloupe or Honeydew Melon: 1 small, cut into 12 wedges
- Prosciutto: 12 thin slices
- Fresh Basil Leaves: 12 large leaves
- Olive Oil: 1 tbsp (optional)
- Black Pepper: To taste

 Prep Time: 10 min

 Cook Time: 0 min

 Serves: 4

Nutritional Info (per serving):

Calories: 120/Protein: 8g/Carbs:10g/Fats: 6g/Fiber: 1g/Sodium: 300mg

DIRECTIONS

Slice the melon into 12 wedges.
Place a basil leaf on top of each melon wedge, then wrap each wedge with a slice of prosciutto.
Arrange the prosciutto-wrapped melon on a serving platter. If desired, drizzle with a small amount of olive oil and sprinkle with freshly ground black pepper.

Eggplant and Tomato Bruschetta

INGREDIENTS

- Eggplant: 1 medium, diced
- Cherry Tomatoes: 1 cup, halved
- Olive Oil: 3 tbsp, divided
- Garlic: 2 cloves, minced
- Balsamic Vinegar: 1 tbsp
- Fresh Basil: 1/4 cup, chopped
- Whole Grain Baguette: 1 small loaf, sliced
- Salt and Pepper: To taste
- Optional: Crumbled feta or Parmesan cheese

Prep Time: 15 min

Cook Time: 20 min

Serves: 4

Nutritional Info (per serving):

Calories: 200/Protein: 4g/Carbs: 20g/Fats: 12g/Fiber: 5g/Sodium: 220mg

DIRECTIONS

Preheat oven to 400°F (200°C). Toss eggplant with 2 tbsp olive oil, salt, and pepper. Roast for 20 minutes until tender.

Combine tomatoes, garlic, balsamic vinegar, 1 tbsp olive oil, and basil. Season with salt and pepper.

Toast baguette slices until golden.

Mix roasted eggplant with tomatoes. Spoon onto toasted bread. Add feta or Parmesan if desired.

Serve immediately.

Seafood Stuffed Mushrooms

INGREDIENTS

- Large Mushrooms: 12, stems removed and chopped
- Shrimp or Crab Meat: 1/2 cup, cooked and chopped
- Olive Oil: 2 tbsp, divided
- Garlic: 2 cloves, minced
- Shallot: 1 small, chopped
- Red Bell Pepper: 1/4 cup, chopped
- Whole Wheat Breadcrumbs: 1/4 cup
- Fresh Parsley: 2 tbsp, chopped
- Lemon Juice: 1 tbsp
- Feta Cheese: 1/4 cup, crumbled (optional)
- Salt and Pepper: To taste
- Paprika: 1/4 tsp (optional)

Prep Time: 20 min

Cook Time: 20 min

Serves: 4

Nutritional Info (per serving):

Calories: 150/Protein: 10g/Carbs:8g/Fats: 10g/Fiber: 2g/Sodium: 250mg

DIRECTIONS

Preheat oven to 375°F (190°C). Clean and chop mushroom stems.

Sauté mushroom stems, garlic, shallot, and bell pepper in 1 tbsp olive oil. Add seafood, breadcrumbs, parsley, lemon juice, salt, and pepper. Cook for 2-3 minutes.

Drizzle the remaining olive oil over the mushroom caps. Fill with the seafood mixture. If using, top with feta and paprika.

Bake for 15-20 minutes until mushrooms are tender and the filling is golden.

Serve warm, garnished with parsley or lemon juice.

Smoked Salmon and Cream Cheese Cucumber Bites

INGREDIENTS

- Cucumber: 1 large, sliced into 16 rounds
- Smoked Salmon: 4 oz, thinly sliced
- Cream Cheese: 1/4 cup, softened
- Lemon Juice: 1 tsp
- Fresh Dill: 2 tbsp, chopped
- Capers: 1 tbsp (optional)
- Black Pepper: To taste

Prep Time: 15 min

Cook Time: 0 min

Serves: 4

Nutritional Info (per serving):

Calories: 100/Protein: 6g/Carbs: 2g/Fats: 7g/Fiber: 0g/Sodium: 280mg

DIRECTIONS

In a small bowl, mix the softened cream cheese with lemon juice, fresh dill, and black pepper until smooth.

Spread a small amount of the cream cheese mixture onto each cucumber slice.

Top each slice with a piece of smoked salmon, folding if necessary.

Place a caper on top of each cucumber bite for added flavor. Garnish with extra dill if desired.

Baba Ganoush with Warm Flatbread

INGREDIENTS

- Eggplant: 1 large
- Tahini: 1/4 cup
- Lemon Juice: 2 tbsp
- Garlic: 2 cloves, minced
- Olive Oil: 2 tbsp
- Salt: 1/2 tsp
- Ground Cumin: 1/2 tsp (optional)
- Smoked Paprika: 1/4 tsp (optional)
- Fresh Parsley: 2 tbsp, chopped (for garnish)

Prep Time: 10 min

Cook Time: 40 min

Serves: 4

Nutritional Info (per serving):

Calories: 220/Protein: 5g/Carbs:25g/Fats: 12g/Fiber: 7g/Sodium: 320mg

DIRECTIONS

Preheat the oven to 400°F (200°C). Pierce the eggplant and roast for 35-40 minutes until soft. Cool, then scoop out the flesh.

Blend eggplant flesh with tahini, lemon juice, garlic, olive oil, salt, cumin, and paprika until smooth.

Warm flatbread in the oven or skillet, brushing with olive oil if desired.

Garnish baba ganoush with parsley and serve with warm flatbread.

Spicy Muhammara
(Red Pepper and Walnut Spread)

INGREDIENTS

- Roasted Red Bell Peppers: 1 cup (about 2 large)
- Walnuts: 1/2 cup, toasted
- Breadcrumbs: 1/4 cup
- Garlic: 2 cloves, minced
- Lemon Juice: 2 tbsp
- Pomegranate Molasses: 1 tbsp (or honey + balsamic vinegar)
- Olive Oil: 2 tbsp
- Ground Cumin: 1 tsp
- Red Pepper Flakes: 1/2 tsp (adjust to taste)
- Paprika: 1/2 tsp
- Salt and Pepper: To taste

 Prep Time: 15 min

 Cook Time: 10 min

 Serves: 4

Nutritional Info (per serving):

Calories: 180/Protein: 4g/Carbs: 12g/Fats: 14g/Fiber: 3g/Sodium: 150mg

DIRECTIONS

Combine all ingredients in a food processor and blend until smooth.
Transfer to a bowl, drizzle with olive oil, and garnish with extra walnuts or paprika if desired.
Serve with pita, veggies, or as a spread.

Mediterranean Cheese Platter with Fig Jam

INGREDIENTS

Cheese:

- Feta Cheese: 4 oz
- Manchego Cheese: 4 oz, sliced
- Goat Cheese: 4 oz

Accompaniments:

- Fig Jam: 1/4 cup
- Mixed Olives: 1/2 cup
- Grapes: 1 cup
- Whole Grain Crackers or Baguette: 8-12 pieces
- Nuts (e.g., almonds, walnuts): 1/4 cup
- Fresh Herbs: For garnish

 Prep Time: 15 min

 Cook Time: 0 min

 Serves: 4

Nutritional Info (per serving):

Calories: 300/Protein: 10g/Carbs:25g/Fats: 18g/Fiber: 3g/Sodium: 450mg

DIRECTIONS

Arrange cheeses, fig jam, olives, grapes, and nuts on a platter. Add crackers or baguette slices.
Garnish with fresh herbs and serve immediately.

Whipped Feta with Honey and Pistachios

INGREDIENTS

- Feta Cheese: 8 oz, crumbled
- Greek Yogurt: 1/4 cup
- Honey: 2 tbsp
- Pistachios: 1/4 cup, chopped
- Olive Oil: 1 tbsp (optional)
- Whole Grain Crackers or Pita Chips: For serving

Prep Time: 10 min

Cook Time: 0 min

Serves: 4

Nutritional Info (per serving):

Calories: 220/Protein: 7g/Carbs: 10g/Fats: 17g/Fiber: 1g/Sodium: 450mg

DIRECTIONS

Blend feta and Greek yogurt in a food processor until smooth.

Transfer to a dish, drizzle with honey, sprinkle with pistachios, and drizzle with olive oil if desired.

Enjoy with crackers or pita chips.

Crispy Polenta Bites with Olive Tapenade

INGREDIENTS

Polenta Bites:

- Polenta: 1 cup, cooked and cooled
- Parmesan Cheese: 1/4 cup, grated (optional)
- Olive Oil: 2 tbsp
- Salt and Pepper: To taste

Olive Tapenade:

- Kalamata Olives: 1/2 cup, pitted
- Green Olives: 1/4 cup, pitted
- Capers: 1 tbsp
- Garlic: 1 clove
- Fresh Parsley: 2 tbsp
- Lemon Juice: 1 tbsp
- Olive Oil: 2 tbsp
- Red Pepper Flakes: 1/4 tsp (optional)

Prep Time: 15 min

Cook Time: 20 min

Serves: 4

Nutritional Info (per serving):

Calories: 180/Protein: 3g/Carbs:20g/Fats: 10g/Fiber: 2g/Sodium: 350mg

DIRECTIONS

Cook polenta, mix in Parmesan (if using), spread in a dish, excellent, and cut into bites.

Preheat oven to 400°F (200°C). Brush polenta bites with olive oil and bake for 15-20 minutes until crispy.

Blend all tapenade ingredients in a food processor until chunky.

Top each polenta bite with tapenade and serve.

Chapter 4
Soup and Salad Recipes

Classic Gazpacho
with Fresh Tomatoes and Cucumber

INGREDIENTS

- Tomatoes: 4 cups, chopped
- Cucumber: 1 large, chopped
- Red Bell Pepper: 1 chopped
- Red Onion: 1/4 cup, chopped
- Garlic: 2 cloves, minced
- Olive Oil: 1/4 cup
- Red Wine Vinegar: 2 tbsp
- Lemon Juice: 1 tbsp
- Salt: 1/2 tsp
- Black Pepper: 1/4 tsp
- Fresh Basil or Parsley: 2 tbsp, chopped (optional)

 Prep Time: 15 min

 Cook Time: 1 hour

 Serves: 4

Nutritional Info (per serving):

Calories: 130/Protein: 2g/Carbs: 12g/Fats: 9g/Fiber: 3g/Sodium: 220mg

DIRECTIONS

Combine all vegetables, olive oil, vinegar, lemon juice, salt, and pepper in a blender. Blend until smooth.
Refrigerate for at least 1 hour to let flavors meld.
Stir and garnish with fresh herbs if desired.

Roasted Red Pepper and Almond Soup

INGREDIENTS

- Roasted Red Bell Peppers: 4, peeled
- Almonds: 1/2 cup, toasted
- Olive Oil: 2 tbsp
- Onion: 1 medium, chopped
- Garlic: 3 cloves, minced
- Vegetable Broth: 4 cups
- Tomato Paste: 2 tbsp
- Smoked Paprika: 1 tsp
- Ground Cumin: 1/2 tsp
- Salt and Pepper: To taste
- Lemon Juice: 1 tbsp
- Fresh Parsley: For garnish (optional)

 Prep Time: 15 min

 Cook Time: 30 min

 Serves: 4

Nutritional Info (per serving):

Calories: 220/Protein: 5g/Carbs:18g/Fats: 14g/Fiber: 3g/Sodium: 450mg

DIRECTIONS

Heat olive oil in a pot. Sauté onion for 5-7 minutes, add garlic, and cook for 1-2 minutes.
Add roasted peppers, almonds, broth, tomato paste, paprika, and cumin. Simmer for 15-20 minutes.
Blend the soup until smooth, stir in lemon juice, and season with salt and pepper. Garnish with parsley if desired.

Lentil and Spinach Soup with Lemon

INGREDIENTS

- Olive Oil: 2 tbsp
- Onion: 1, chopped
- Carrots: 2 diced
- Celery: 2 stalks, diced
- Garlic: 3 cloves, minced
- Lentils: 1 cup, rinsed
- Vegetable Broth: 4 cups
- Water: 2 cups
- Spinach: 4 cups, packed
- Lemon Juice: 2 tbsp
- Lemon Zest: 1 tsp
- Ground Cumin: 1 tsp
- Salt and Pepper: To taste
- Fresh Parsley: For garnish (optional)

Prep Time: 10 min   Cook Time: 30 min   Serves: 4

Nutritional Info (per serving):

Calories: 220/Protein: 10g/Carbs: 30g/Fats: 7g/Fiber: 10g/Sodium: 400mg

DIRECTIONS

Heat olive oil in a pot, sauté onion, carrots, and celery for 5-7 minutes. Add garlic and cook for 1-2 minutes.
Add lentils, broth, and water. Simmer for 20-25 minutes until lentils are tender.
Stir in spinach, lemon juice, zest, and cumin. Cook until spinach wilts, then season with salt and pepper.
Garnish with parsley and serve.

Creamy Tomato Basil Soup with Roasted Garlic

INGREDIENTS

- Tomatoes: 4 cups, chopped
- Garlic: 1 whole head
- Olive Oil: 2 tbsp, divided
- Onion: 1, chopped
- Vegetable Broth: 4 cups
- Fresh Basil: 1/2 cup, chopped
- Tomato Paste: 2 tbsp
- Salt and Pepper: To taste
- Greek Yogurt: 1/4 cup (optional for creaminess)

Prep Time: 10 min   Cook Time: 40 min   Serves: 4

Nutritional Info (per serving):

Calories: 180/Protein: 4g/Carbs:28g/Fats: 8g/Fiber: 6g/Sodium: 400mg

DIRECTIONS

Preheat the oven to 400°F (200°C). Slice the top off the garlic head, drizzle with olive oil, wrap in foil, and roast for 30 minutes. Let it cool, then squeeze out the cloves.
In a pot, heat 1 tbsp olive oil. Sauté onion until soft. Add tomatoes, roasted garlic, broth, basil, and tomato paste. Simmer for 20 minutes.
Blend until smooth. Stir in Greek yogurt if using. Season with salt and pepper.

Creamy Cauliflower and Leek Soup with Parmesan

INGREDIENTS

- Olive Oil: 2 tbsp
- Leeks: 2, sliced
- Garlic: 3 cloves, minced
- Cauliflower: 1 large head, chopped
- Vegetable Broth: 4 cups
- Bay Leaf: 1
- Salt and Pepper: To taste
- Parmesan Cheese: 1/4 cup, grated
- Greek Yogurt: 1/2 cup (optional)
- Fresh Parsley: For garnish (optional)

 Prep Time: 15 min

Cook Time: 30 min

 Serves: 4

Nutritional Info (per serving):

Calories: 220/Protein: 8g/Carbs: 15g/Fats: 12g/Fiber: 4g/Sodium: 450mg

DIRECTIONS

Heat olive oil in a pot and sauté leeks for 5-7 minutes. Add garlic and cook for 1-2 minutes.

Add cauliflower, broth, and bay leaf. Simmer for 20 minutes until cauliflower is tender.

Remove the bay leaf and blend the soup until smooth. Stir in Parmesan and Greek yogurt if using. Season with salt and pepper.

Garnish with parsley and serve warm.

Butternut Squash and Sage Soup

INGREDIENTS

- Butternut Squash: 1 medium, diced (about 4 cups)
- Olive Oil: 2 tbsp
- Onion: 1, chopped
- Garlic: 3 cloves, minced
- Fresh Sage: 1 tbsp, chopped (plus more for garnish)
- Vegetable Broth: 4 cups
- Salt and Pepper: To taste
- Greek Yogurt: 1/4 cup (optional)

 Prep Time: 15 min

 Cook Time: 30 min

 Serves: 4

Nutritional Info (per serving):

Calories: 180/Protein: 3g/Carbs:28g/Fats: 7g/Fiber: 5g/Sodium: 400mg

DIRECTIONS

Heat olive oil in a pot, sauté onion for 5-7 minutes. Add garlic and sage, cook for 1-2 minutes.

Add squash and broth. Simmer for 20-25 minutes until tender. Blend until smooth. Stir in Greek yogurt if desired. Season with salt and pepper.

Garnish with sage and serve warm.

Tuscan White Bean and Kale Soup

INGREDIENTS

- Olive Oil: 2 tbsp
- Onion: 1, chopped
- Carrots: 2 diced
- Garlic: 3 cloves, minced
- White Beans: 2 cups (or one can, drained)
- Vegetable Broth: 4 cups
- Kale: 4 cups, chopped
- Salt and Pepper: To taste
- Parmesan Cheese: 1/4 cup, grated (optional)

 Prep Time: 10 min   Cook Time: 30 min   Serves: 4

Nutritional Info (per serving):

Calories: 220/Protein: 10g/Carbs: 30g/Fats: 7g/Fiber: 10g/Sodium: 450mg

DIRECTIONS

Heat olive oil in a pot, sauté onion and carrots for 5 minutes. Add garlic and cook for 1 minute.

Add beans, broth, and seasonings. Simmer for 15 minutes.

Stir in kale and cook until wilted about 5 minutes.

Garnish with Parmesan if desired, and serve.

Caramelized Onion and Fennel Soup

INGREDIENTS

- Olive Oil: 2 tbsp
- Onions: 4, thinly sliced
- Fennel Bulb: 1, thinly sliced
- Garlic: 3 cloves, minced
- Fresh Thyme: 1 tsp
- Bay Leaf: 1
- Vegetable Broth: 4 cups
- White Wine: 1/2 cup (optional)
- Salt and Pepper: To taste
- Parmesan Cheese: 1/4 cup, grated (optional)
- Fresh Parsley: For garnish (optional)

 Prep Time: 15 min   Cook Time: 45 min   Serves: 4

Nutritional Info (per serving):

Calories: 180/Protein: 4g/Carbs:22g/Fats: 9g/Fiber: 5g/Sodium: 450mg

DIRECTIONS

Heat olive oil in a pot over medium heat. Add onions and fennel, cooking for 20-25 minutes until caramelized.

Stir in garlic, thyme, and bay leaf. Cook for 1-2 minutes.

Add white wine (if using), cook for 2-3 minutes. Add broth and simmer for 15-20 minutes.

Season with salt and pepper. Garnish with Parmesan and parsley if desired.
*

Turkish Red Lentil Soup with Mint Oil

INGREDIENTS

- Red Lentils: 1 cup, rinsed
- Olive Oil: 2 tbsp, divided
- Onion: 1, chopped
- Carrots: 2 diced
- Garlic: 3 cloves, minced
- Tomato Paste: 2 tbsp
- Ground Cumin: 1 tsp
- Paprika: 1 tsp
- Vegetable Broth: 4 cups
- Water: 2 cups
- Lemon Juice: 2 tbsp
- Dried Mint: 1 tbsp
- Salt and Pepper: To taste

Prep Time: 10 min

Cook Time: 30 min

Serves: 4

Nutritional Info (per serving):

Calories: 220/Protein: 10g/Carbs: 30g/Fats:8g/Fiber: 8g/Sodium: 450mg

DIRECTIONS

Heat 1 tbsp olive oil in a pot. Sauté onion and carrots for 5-7 minutes. Add garlic, tomato paste, cumin, and paprika; cook 1-2 minutes.
Add lentils, broth, and water. Simmer for 20-25 minutes until lentils are tender. Blend soup until smooth. Stir in lemon juice, salt, and pepper.
Heat 1 tbsp olive oil in a small skillet. Add dried mint and cook for 1 minute. Drizzle soup with mint oil and serve.

Grilled Peach and Burrata Salad
with Balsamic Glaze

INGREDIENTS

- Peaches: 4, halved and pitted
- Olive Oil: 2 tbsp
- Burrata Cheese: 8 oz, torn
- Mixed Greens: 4 cups
- Fresh Basil: 1/4 cup, chopped
- Balsamic Glaze: 2 tbsp
- Salt and Pepper: To taste

Prep Time: 10 min

Cook Time: 10 min

Serves: 4

Nutritional Info (per serving):

Calories: 220/Protein: 8g/Carbs:16g/Fats: 14g/Fiber: 2g/Sodium: 150mg

DIRECTIONS

Brush peaches with olive oil and grill cut side down for 3-4 minutes until softened.
Arrange mixed greens on a platter and top with grilled peaches, Burrata, and basil.
Drizzle with balsamic glaze, season with salt and pepper, and serve.

Quinoa Tabbouleh with Fresh Herbs

INGREDIENTS

- Quinoa: 1 cup
- Water: 2 cups
- Fresh Parsley: 1 cup, chopped
- Fresh Mint: 1/2 cup, chopped
- Cherry Tomatoes: 1 cup, quartered
- Cucumber: 1, diced
- Green Onions: 4, sliced
- Lemon Juice: 1/4 cup
- Olive Oil: 1/4 cup
- Salt and Pepper: To taste

 Prep Time: 15 min

 Cook Time: 15 min

 Serves: 4

Nutritional Info (per serving):

Calories: 200/Protein: 5g/Carbs: 28g/Fats:8g/Fiber: 4g/Sodium: 180mg

DIRECTIONS

Rinse quinoa and cook with water for 15 minutes until tender. Let cool.
Chop parsley, mint, tomatoes, cucumber, and green onions.
Combine quinoa, vegetables, lemon juice, olive oil, salt, and pepper. Toss to mix.
Serve immediately or chill before serving.

Spinach and Orzo Salad with Sundried Tomatoes

INGREDIENTS

- Orzo: 1 cup
- Spinach: 4 cups, chopped
- Sundried Tomatoes: 1/2 cup, chopped
- Feta Cheese: 1/2 cup, crumbled
- Pine Nuts: 1/4 cup, toasted
- Fresh Basil: 1/4 cup, chopped
- Olive Oil: 2 tbsp
- Lemon Juice: 2 tbsp
- Garlic: 1 clove, minced
- Salt and Pepper: To taste

 Prep Time: 10 min

 Cook Time: 15 min

 Serves: 4

Nutritional Info (per serving):

Calories: 320/Protein: 8g/Carbs:35g/Fats: 16g/Fiber: 4g/Sodium: 320mg

DIRECTIONS

Boil orzo until al dente, drain, and cool slightly. Whisk together olive oil, lemon juice, garlic, salt, and pepper.
Combine orzo, spinach, sundried tomatoes, feta, pine nuts, and basil in a large bowl.
Toss salad with dressing and serve immediately, or chill for an hour.

Roasted Beet and Arugula Salad with Goat Cheese

INGREDIENTS

- Beets: 4 medium, trimmed
- Arugula: 4 cups
- Goat Cheese: 1/2 cup, crumbled
- Walnuts: 1/4 cup, toasted
- Olive Oil: 3 tbsp, divided
- Balsamic Vinegar: 2 tbsp
- Honey: 1 tsp
- Salt and Pepper: To taste

 Prep Time: 15 min   Cook Time: 40 min   Serves: 4

Nutritional Info (per serving):

Calories: 320/Protein: 6g/Carbs: 18g/Fats:16g/Fiber: 4g/Sodium: 200mg

DIRECTIONS

Preheat oven to 400°F (200°C). Wrap beets in foil and roast for 35-40 minutes. Cool, peel, and slice.
Whisk 2 tbsp olive oil, balsamic vinegar, honey, salt, and pepper.
Toss arugula with 1 tbsp olive oil. Top with beets, goat cheese, and walnuts.
Drizzle with dressing, toss gently, and serve.

Watermelon, Cucumber, and Feta Salad

INGREDIENTS

- Watermelon: 4 cups, cubed
- Cucumber: 1 large, diced
- Feta Cheese: 1/2 cup, crumbled
- Fresh Mint: 1/4 cup, chopped
- Olive Oil: 2 tablespoons
- Lime Juice: 1 tablespoon
- Salt and Pepper: To taste

 Prep Time: 10 min   Cook Time: 0 min   Serves: 4

Nutritional Info (per serving):

Calories: 150/Protein: 4g/Carbs:14g/Fats: 9g/Fiber: 1g/Sodium: 220mg

DIRECTIONS

Combine the cubed watermelon, diced cucumber, crumbled feta cheese, and chopped mint in a large bowl.
Whisk together olive oil, lime juice, salt, and pepper in a small bowl.
Drizzle the dressing over the watermelon mixture and toss gently to combine.
Serve immediately, or chill in the refrigerator for 15 minutes before serving for a refreshing, excellent salad.

Shaved Fennel and Orange Salad with Olives and Dill

INGREDIENTS

- Fennel Bulb: 1, thinly sliced
- Oranges: 2, segmented
- Kalamata Olives: 1/2 cup, halved
- Fresh Dill: 1/4 cup, chopped
- Olive Oil: 2 tbsp
- Lemon Juice: 1 tbsp
- Salt and Pepper: To taste

Prep Time: 15 min

Cook Time: 0 min

Serves: 4

Nutritional Info (per serving):

Calories: 150/Protein: 2g/Carbs: 17g/Fats:9g/Fiber: 5g/Sodium: 280mg

DIRECTIONS

Combine shaved fennel, orange segments, olives, and dill in a bowl.
Whisk together olive oil, lemon juice, salt, and pepper.
Drizzle dressing over salad, toss gently, and serve.

Warm Barley and Roasted Vegetable Salad

INGREDIENTS

- Pearl Barley: 1 cup
- Water or Vegetable Broth: 3 cups
- Red Bell Pepper: 1 diced
- Zucchini: 1 diced
- Eggplant: 1 small, diced
- Cherry Tomatoes: 1 cup, halved
- Olive Oil: 3 tbsp, divided
- Garlic: 2 cloves, minced
- Fresh Parsley: 1/4 cup, chopped
- Lemon Juice: 2 tbsp
- Salt and Pepper: To taste

Prep Time: 15 min

Cook Time: 40 min

Serves: 4

Nutritional Info (per serving):

Calories: 300/Protein: 7g/Carbs:50g/Fats: 10g/Fiber: 10g/Sodium: 250mg

DIRECTIONS

Boil barley in water or broth for 25-30 minutes until tender. Drain and set aside.
Preheat the oven to 400°F (200°C). Toss the bell pepper, zucchini, eggplant, and tomatoes with two tablespoons of olive oil, salt, and pepper. Roast for 20-25 minutes.
Combine cooked barley, roasted vegetables, garlic, parsley, lemon juice, and olive oil. Toss to mix.
Serve warm, garnished with extra parsley if desired.

Avocado and Tomato Salad
with Basil and Mozzarella

INGREDIENTS

- Avocado: 2, diced
- Cherry Tomatoes: 1 cup, halved
- Fresh Mozzarella: 8 oz, diced
- Fresh Basil: 1/4 cup, chopped
- Olive Oil: 2 tbsp
- Balsamic Vinegar: 1 tbsp
- Lemon Juice: 1 tbsp
- Salt and Pepper: To taste
- Optional: Red pepper flakes

Prep Time: 15 min

Cook Time: 0 min

Serves: 4

Nutritional Info (per serving):

Calories: 250/Protein: 8g/Carbs: 10g/Fats:21g/Fiber: 5g/Sodium: 150mg

DIRECTIONS

Toss avocado, tomatoes, mozzarella, and basil in a large bowl.
Whisk together olive oil, balsamic vinegar, lemon juice, salt, and pepper.
Drizzle dressing over the salad, toss gently, and serve immediately.

Grilled Asparagus and Quinoa Salad
with Feta and Mint

INGREDIENTS

- Quinoa: 1 cup
- Water or Vegetable Broth: 2 cups
- Asparagus: 1 bunch, trimmed
- Olive Oil: 2 tbsp, divided
- Feta Cheese: 1/2 cup, crumbled
- Fresh Mint: 1/4 cup, chopped
- Lemon Juice: 2 tbsp
- Lemon Zest: 1 tsp
- Salt and Pepper: To taste

Prep Time: 15 min

Cook Time: 20 min

Serves: 4

Nutritional Info (per serving):

Calories: 250/Protein: 8g/Carbs:28g/Fats: 12g/Fiber: 5g/Sodium: 200mg

DIRECTIONS

Cook quinoa in water or broth for 15 minutes, until tender. Set aside to cool.
Toss asparagus with 1 tbsp olive oil, salt, and pepper. Grill for 5-7 minutes until slightly charred. Cut into bite-sized pieces.
Combine the quinoa, grilled asparagus, feta, and mint in a bowl. Whisk in the remaining olive oil, lemon juice, lemon zest, salt, and pepper. Drizzle over the salad, toss gently, and serve.

Chapter 5
Grains, Pasta, and Rice Recipes

Tuscan Farro Salad with Roasted Vegetables

INGREDIENTS

- Farro: 1 cup
- Water or Vegetable Broth: 2 1/2 cups
- Red Bell Pepper: 1 diced
- Zucchini: 1 diced
- Cherry Tomatoes: 1 cup, halved
- Red Onion: 1/2, sliced
- Olive Oil: 3 tbsp, divided
- Fresh Basil: 1/4 cup, chopped
- Fresh Parsley: 1/4 cup, chopped
- Balsamic Vinegar: 2 tbsp
- Salt and Pepper: To taste

 Prep Time: 15 min

 Cook Time: 30 min

 Serves: 4

Nutritional Info (per serving):

Calories: 320/Protein: 8g/Carbs: 44g/Fats:12g/Fiber: 7g/Sodium: 220mg

DIRECTIONS

Cook farro in boiling water or broth for 25-30 minutes until tender. Drain and cool.

Preheat oven to 400°F (200°C). Toss vegetables with 2 tbsp olive oil, salt, and pepper. Roast for 20-25 minutes until tender.

Combine cooked farro, roasted vegetables, basil, and parsley in a large bowl.

Whisk the remaining olive oil and balsamic vinegar. Drizzle over salad, toss, and serve.

Lemon Basil Risotto with Asparagus

INGREDIENTS

- Arborio Rice: 1 cup
- Asparagus: 1 bunch, trimmed and cut into 1-inch pieces
- Vegetable Broth: 4 cups, warmed
- Olive Oil: 2 tbsp
- Onion: 1 small, finely chopped
- Garlic: 2 cloves, minced
- Lemon Juice: 2 tbsp
- Lemon Zest: 1 tsp
- Fresh Basil: 1/4 cup, chopped
- Parmesan Cheese: 1/4 cup, grated
- Salt and Pepper: To taste

 Prep Time: 10 min

 Cook Time: 30 min

 Serves: 4

Nutritional Info (per serving):

Calories: 280/Protein: 7g/Carbs:45g/Fats: 8g/Fiber: 3g/Sodium: 400mg

DIRECTIONS

Heat olive oil in a skillet. Sauté onion and garlic until softened.

Add Arborio rice, stirring to coat. Gradually add warm broth, 1 cup at a time, stirring until absorbed.

Stir in asparagus during the last 10 minutes of cooking.

Once rice is creamy and tender, stir in lemon juice, zest, basil, and Parmesan. Season with salt and pepper.

Serve warm, garnished with extra basil or Parmesan if desired.

Saffron-Infused Paella with Mixed Seafood

INGREDIENTS

- Olive Oil: 2 tbsp
- Onion: 1 small, chopped
- Garlic: 3 cloves, minced
- Red Bell Pepper: 1 diced
- Arborio Rice: 1 1/2 cups
- Saffron: 1/2 tsp, soaked in warm water
- Broth: 4 cups, warm
- Mixed Seafood: 1 lb (shrimp, mussels, clams, squid)
- Peas: 1/2 cup, frozen
- Fresh Parsley: 1/4 cup, chopped
- Lemon Wedges: For serving
- Salt and Pepper: To taste

 Prep Time: 15 min

 Cook Time: 35 min

Serves: 4

Nutritional Info (per serving):

Calories: 450/Protein: 30g/Carbs: 50g/Fats:12g/Fiber: 4g/Sodium: 750mg

DIRECTIONS

Heat olive oil, sauté onion, garlic, and bell pepper until soft.
Add rice and saffron. Gradually stir in broth until absorbed.
Add seafood and peas, and cook until the seafood is done and the rice is tender.
Garnish with parsley and lemon wedges.

Baked Brown Rice Pilaf with Lemon and Thyme

INGREDIENTS

- Brown Rice: 1 cup
- Vegetable Broth: 2 1/2 cups
- Olive Oil: 2 tbsp
- Onion: 1 small, chopped
- Garlic: 2 cloves, minced
- Fresh Thyme: 1 tbsp (or 1 tsp dried thyme)
- Lemon Zest: 1 tsp
- Lemon Juice: 1 tbsp
- Salt and Pepper: To taste
- Fresh Parsley: 2 tbsp, chopped (optional)

 Prep Time: 10 min

 Cook Time: 50 min

 Serves: 4

Nutritional Info (per serving):

Calories: 230/Protein: 4g/Carbs:40g/Fats: 7g/Fiber: 3g/Sodium: 250mg

DIRECTIONS

Preheat oven to 375°F (190°C).
Heat olive oil in an oven-safe skillet. Sauté onion and garlic until soft.
Stir in brown rice, broth, thyme, lemon zest, lemon juice, salt, and pepper. Bring to a simmer.
Cover and bake for 45-50 minutes until rice is tender.
Fluff with a fork, garnish with parsley if desired, and serve warm.

Pesto Pasta Salad
with Pine Nuts and Cherry Tomatoes

INGREDIENTS

- Whole Wheat Pasta: 8 oz
- Cherry Tomatoes: 1 cup, halved
- Pine Nuts: 1/4 cup, toasted
- Fresh Basil: 1/2 cup, packed
- Parmesan Cheese: 1/4 cup, grated
- Garlic: 1 clove
- Olive Oil: 1/4 cup
- Lemon Juice: 1 tbsp
- Salt and Pepper: To taste

Prep Time: 15 min

Cook Time: 10 min

Serves: 4

Nutritional Info (per serving):

Calories: 350/Protein: 10g/Carbs: 40g/Fats:18g/Fiber: 5g/Sodium: 180mg

DIRECTIONS

Cook pasta until al dente. Drain and cool.

Blend basil, Parmesan, garlic, olive oil, lemon juice, salt, and pepper in a food processor.

Toss pasta, cherry tomatoes, pine nuts, and pesto until well combined.

Serve chilled or at room temperature, garnish as desired.

Pearl Couscous with Mint and Pomegranate

INGREDIENTS

- Pearl Couscous: 1 cup
- Water or Vegetable Broth: 1 1/4 cups
- Pomegranate Seeds: 1/2 cup
- Fresh Mint: 1/4 cup, chopped
- Olive Oil: 2 tbsp
- Lemon Juice: 1 tbsp
- Salt and Pepper: To taste

Prep Time: 10 min

Cook Time: 15 min

Serves: 4

Nutritional Info (per serving):

Calories: 220/Protein: 4g/Carbs:32g/Fats: 9g/Fiber: 3g/Sodium: 150mg

DIRECTIONS

Boil water or broth, add couscous, and simmer for 10 minutes until tender. Fluff and cool slightly.

Combine couscous, pomegranate seeds, and mint in a bowl.

Whisk together olive oil, lemon juice, salt, and pepper. Drizzle over salad and toss.

Serve at room temperature or chilled, garnish with nuts if desired.

Mediterranean Quinoa
with Sun-Dried Tomatoes and Feta

INGREDIENTS

- Quinoa: 1 cup
- Water or Vegetable Broth: 2 cups
- Sun-Dried Tomatoes: 1/2 cup, chopped
- Feta Cheese: 1/2 cup, crumbled
- Kalamata Olives: 1/4 cup, sliced
- Fresh Basil: 1/4 cup, chopped
- Olive Oil: 2 tbsp
- Lemon Juice: 1 tbsp
- Garlic: 1 clove, minced
- Salt and Pepper: To taste

 Prep Time: 10 min

 Cook Time: 15 min

Serves: 4

Nutritional Info (per serving):

Calories: 290/Protein: 8g/Carbs: 30g/Fats:15g/Fiber: 4g/Sodium: 350mg

DIRECTIONS

Boil water or broth, add quinoa, cover, and simmer for 15 minutes. Fluff and set aside.
Combine cooked quinoa, sun-dried tomatoes, feta, olives, and basil in a bowl.
Whisk olive oil, lemon juice, garlic, salt, and pepper. Drizzle over salad and toss.
Serve warm or chilled.

Spanish Rice with Chorizo and Peppers

INGREDIENTS

- Olive Oil: 2 tbsp
- Chorizo: 6 oz, sliced
- Onion: 1 chopped
- Red Bell Pepper: 1 chopped
- Green Bell Pepper: 1, chopped
- Garlic: 2 cloves, minced
- Long Grain Rice: 1 cup
- Diced Tomatoes: 1 can (14.5 oz)
- Chicken or Vegetable Broth: 2 cups
- Smoked Paprika: 1 tsp
- Ground Cumin: 1/2 tsp
- Salt and Pepper: To taste
- Fresh Parsley: 1/4 cup, chopped (optional)

 Prep Time: 10 min

 Cook Time: 25 min

 Serves: 4

Nutritional Info (per serving):

Calories: 380/Protein: 14g/Carbs:40g/Fats: 18g/Fiber: 4g/Sodium: 750mg

DIRECTIONS

Heat olive oil in a skillet. Cook chorizo until browned, then remove.
Sauté onion, peppers, and garlic in the same skillet until softened.
Stir in rice, smoked paprika, cumin, salt, and pepper. Cook briefly.
Add diced tomatoes and broth. Simmer covered for 15-20 minutes until rice is tender.
Stir in cooked chorizo and garnish with parsley. Serve warm.

Creamy Polenta with Wild Mushrooms and Herbs

INGREDIENTS

Polenta:

- Polenta: 1 cup
- Water or Broth: 4 cups
- Parmesan Cheese: 1/4 cup, grated (optional)
- Olive Oil or Butter: 1 tbsp
- Salt: To taste

Mushrooms:

- Wild Mushrooms: 1 lb, sliced
- Olive Oil: 2 tbsp
- Garlic: 2 cloves, minced
- Fresh Thyme: 1 tbsp, chopped
- Fresh Parsley: 1/4 cup, chopped
- Salt and Pepper: To taste

 Prep Time: 10 min

 Cook Time: 30 min

 Serves: 4

Nutritional Info (per serving):

Calories: 260/Protein: 6g/Carbs: 35g/Fats:10g/Fiber: 4g/Sodium: 200mg

DIRECTIONS

Bring water or broth to a boil. Whisk in polenta, reduce heat, and cook for 25-30 minutes until creamy. Stir in olive oil or butter and Parmesan if using. Season with salt.

Heat olive oil in a skillet. Add garlic sauté for 1-2 minutes. Add mushrooms and cook until golden. Stir in thyme, salt, and pepper.

Serve polenta topped with mushrooms. Garnish with parsley.

Lemon Garlic Orzo with Spinach and Feta

INGREDIENTS

- Orzo: 1 cup
- Olive Oil: 2 tbsp
- Garlic: 3 cloves, minced
- Spinach: 4 cups
- Lemon Zest: 1 tsp
- Lemon Juice: 2 tbsp
- Feta Cheese: 1/2 cup, crumbled
- Fresh Parsley: 1/4 cup, chopped
- Salt and Pepper: To taste
- Red Pepper Flakes: Optional, to taste

 Prep Time: 10 min

 Cook Time: 15 min

 Serves: 4

Nutritional Info (per serving):

Calories: 250/Protein: 8g/Carbs:32g/Fats: 10g/Fiber: 3g/Sodium: 320mg

DIRECTIONS

Boil orzo until al dente, then drain.

Heat olive oil in a skillet. Sauté garlic for 1 minute, add spinach and cook until wilted.

Add the cooked orzo to the skillet with the spinach. Stir in lemon zest, lemon juice, salt, pepper, and red pepper flakes if using.

Remove from heat, stir in crumbled feta cheese and chopped parsley. Serve warm.

Farfalle with Spinach and Ricotta

INGREDIENTS

- Farfalle Pasta: 8 oz
- Olive Oil: 2 tbsp
- Garlic: 2 cloves, minced
- Spinach: 4 cups, packed
- Ricotta Cheese: 1/2 cup
- Parmesan Cheese: 1/4 cup, grated (optional)
- Lemon Zest: 1 tsp
- Fresh Basil: 1/4 cup, chopped
- Salt and Pepper: To taste
- Red Pepper Flakes: Optional, to taste

 Prep Time: 10 min

 Cook Time: 15 min

 Serves: 4

Nutritional Info (per serving):

Calories: 320/Protein: 12g/Carbs: 40g/Fats:14g/Fiber: 4g/Sodium: 200mg

DIRECTIONS

Boil farfalle until al dente. Drain and set aside.

Heat olive oil in a skillet. Sauté garlic for 1 minute, add spinach and cook until wilted.

Add the cooked farfalle to the skillet with the spinach. Stir in ricotta cheese, lemon zest, salt, pepper, and red pepper flakes if using. Mix well until the pasta is evenly coated.

Serve warm, garnished with extra basil or Parmesan if desired.

Red Lentil Pasta with Tomato and Basil Sauce

INGREDIENTS

- Red Lentil Pasta: 8 oz
- Olive Oil: 2 tbsp
- Garlic: 3 cloves, minced
- Onion: 1 small, chopped
- Crushed Tomatoes: 1 can (14.5 oz)
- Tomato Paste: 2 tbsp
- Fresh Basil: 1/4 cup, chopped
- Salt and Pepper: To taste
- Red Pepper Flakes: Optional
- Parmesan Cheese: 1/4 cup, grated (optional)

 Prep Time: 10 min

 Cook Time: 20 min

 Serves: 4

Nutritional Info (per serving):

Calories: 320/Protein: 18g/Carbs:46g/Fats: 8g/Fiber: 8g/Sodium: 280mg

DIRECTIONS

Boil pasta until al dente. Drain and set aside.

Sauté onion in olive oil until soft, then add garlic and cook for 1 minute. Stir in tomatoes, tomato paste, salt, pepper, and red pepper flakes. Simmer for 10-15 minutes.

Toss pasta with sauce, stir in basil, and garnish with Parmesan if desired.

Whole Wheat Pasta with Eggplant and Olive Tapenade

INGREDIENTS

- Whole Wheat Pasta: 8 oz
- Eggplant: 1 medium, diced
- Olive Oil: 3 tbsp
- Garlic: 3 cloves, minced
- Olive Tapenade: 1/2 cup
- Cherry Tomatoes: 1 cup, halved
- Fresh Basil: 1/4 cup, chopped
- Salt and Pepper: To taste
- Parmesan Cheese: 1/4 cup, grated (optional)

 Prep Time: 15 min

 Cook Time: 25 min

 Serves: 4

Nutritional Info (per serving):

Calories: 360/Protein: 10g/Carbs: 45g/Fats:15g/Fiber: 8g/Sodium: 400mg

DIRECTIONS

Boil pasta until al dente, then drain.

Sauté diced eggplant in 2 tbsp olive oil until tender and golden. Set aside.

In the same skillet, add 1 tbsp olive oil. Sauté garlic for 1 minute, then add tomatoes and cook until softened.

Add eggplant, olive tapenade, and cooked pasta to the skillet. Toss to combine, and season with salt and pepper.

Stir in fresh basil and garnish with Parmesan cheese if desired. Serve warm.

Quinoa Stuffed Bell Peppers

INGREDIENTS

- Bell Peppers: 4, tops removed
- Quinoa: 1 cup
- Water/Broth: 2 cups
- Olive Oil: 2 tbsp
- Onion: 1 small, chopped
- Garlic: 3 cloves, minced
- Zucchini: 1 small, diced
- Cherry Tomatoes: 1 cup, halved
- Kalamata Olives: 1/4 cup, chopped
- Feta Cheese: 1/2 cup, crumbled
- Fresh Herbs: 1/4 cup, chopped (parsley, basil)
- Salt, Pepper, Red Pepper Flakes: To taste

 Prep Time: 10 min

 Cook Time: 20 min

 Serves: 4

Nutritional Info (per serving):

Calories: 280/Protein: 8g/Carbs:35g/Fats: 12g/Fiber: 7g/Sodium: 300mg

DIRECTIONS

Boil quinoa in water/broth for 15 minutes. Set aside.

Sauté onion, garlic, and zucchini in olive oil. Add tomatoes, olives, quinoa, and feta. Season with herbs, salt, and pepper.

Fill peppers with quinoa mixture. Bake at 375°F (190°C) for 25-30 minutes, covered with foil.

Serve warm with extra herbs.

Moroccan Couscous
with Dried Apricots and Almonds

INGREDIENTS

- Couscous: 1 cup
- Water/Broth: 1 1/4 cups
- Olive Oil: 2 tbsp
- Onion: 1 small, chopped
- Garlic: 2 cloves, minced
- Spices (Cumin, Cinnamon, Turmeric): 1/2 tsp each
- Dried Apricots: 1/2 cup, chopped
- Almonds: 1/4 cup, sliced
- Fresh Herbs: 1/4 cup, chopped
- Lemon Juice: 1 tbsp

 Prep Time: 5 min

 Cook Time: 10 min

 Serves: 4

Nutritional Info (per serving):

Calories: 250/Protein: 6g/Carbs: 40g/Fats:8g/Fiber: 4g/Sodium: 100mg

DIRECTIONS

Bring water or broth to a boil. Stir in couscous, cover, and remove from heat. Let it sit for 5 minutes, then fluff it with a fork.

Heat olive oil in a skillet, sauté onion for 3-4 minutes. Add garlic and spices, and cook for 1 minute.

Mix couscous, apricots, almonds, herbs, and lemon juice into the skillet. Season with salt and pepper. Serve warm or at room temperature.

Multi-Grain Pilaf with Dates and Pine Nuts

INGREDIENTS

- Brown Rice: 1/2 cup
- Quinoa: 1/4 cup
- Bulgur: 1/4 cup
- Water/Broth: 2 cups
- Olive Oil: 2 tbsp
- Onion: 1 small, chopped
- Garlic: 2 cloves, minced
- Dates: 1/4 cup, chopped
- Pine Nuts: 1/4 cup, toasted
- Fresh Parsley: 1/4 cup, chopped
- Salt and Pepper: To taste
- Optional: Lemon Zest, Cinnamon/Allspice

 Prep Time: 10 min

 Cook Time: 30 min

 Serves: 4

Nutritional Info (per serving):

Calories: 300/Protein: 6g/Carbs:45g/Fats: 12g/Fiber: 6g/Sodium: 150mg

DIRECTIONS

Boil grains in water or broth for 25-30 minutes until tender. Fluff with a fork.

Sauté onion in olive oil until soft. Add garlic and cook for 1 minute.

Mix cooked grains, dates, pine nuts, and parsley with the sautéed onions. Season with salt, pepper, and optional spices.

Serve warm, garnished with extra parsley or pine nuts.

Artichoke and Olive Orzo Salad

INGREDIENTS

- Orzo: 1 cup
- Artichoke Hearts: 1 cup, chopped
- Kalamata Olives: 1/2 cup, sliced
- Cherry Tomatoes: 1 cup, halved
- Red Onion: 1/4 cup, chopped
- Fresh Parsley and Basil: 1/4 cup each, chopped
- Olive Oil: 3 tbsp
- Lemon Juice: 2 tbsp
- Garlic: 1 clove, minced
- Feta Cheese: 1/4 cup, crumbled (optional)
- Salt and Pepper: To taste

 Prep Time: 10 min

 Cook Time: 10 min

 Serves: 4

Nutritional Info (per serving):

Calories: 280/Protein: 6g/Carbs: 36g/Fats: 14g/Fiber: 4g/Sodium: 400mg

DIRECTIONS

Boil orzo until al dente. Drain and cool.

Whisk together olive oil, lemon juice, garlic, salt, and pepper.

Combine orzo, artichokes, olives, tomatoes, onion, parsley, and basil. Toss with dressing.

Top with feta if desired. Serve chilled or at room temperature.

Creamy Farro Risotto with Mushrooms and Spinach

INGREDIENTS

- Farro: 1 cup
- Olive Oil: 2 tbsp
- Onion: 1 small, chopped
- Garlic: 2 cloves, minced
- Mushrooms: 2 cups, sliced
- Vegetable Broth: 4 cups, warm
- White Wine: 1/2 cup (optional)
- Spinach: 2 cups, packed
- Parmesan Cheese: 1/4 cup, grated (optional)
- Salt and Pepper: To taste
- Fresh Thyme: 1 tsp, chopped (optional)

 Prep Time: 10 min

 Cook Time: 40 min

 Serves: 4

Nutritional Info (per serving):

Calories: 320/Protein: 10g/Carbs:50g/Fats: 10g/Fiber: 8g/Sodium: 300mg

DIRECTIONS

Boil farro in water until tender, about 20 minutes. Drain.

Heat olive oil in a skillet, sauté onion until soft. Add garlic and mushrooms, and cook until browned. Add cooked farro to the skillet. Stir in white wine (if using) until absorbed. Gradually add warm broth, stirring until creamy.

Stir in spinach until wilted. Season with salt, pepper, and thyme. Add Parmesan if desired.

Serve warm, garnished with extra cheese or herbs if desired.

Chapter 6
Fish and Seafood

Grilled Salmon with Dill and Lemon

INGREDIENTS

- Salmon Fillets: 4 (6 oz each)
- Olive Oil: 2 tbsp
- Lemon Juice: 2 tbsp
- Fresh Dill: 2 tbsp, chopped
- Garlic: 2 cloves, minced
- Salt and Pepper: To taste
- Lemon Slices: For garnish

Prep Time: 10 min

Cook Time: 10 min

Serves: 4

Nutritional Info (per serving):

Calories: 320/Protein: 34g/Carbs: 1g/Fats: 20g/Fiber: 0g/Sodium: 220mg

DIRECTIONS

Mix olive oil, lemon juice, dill, garlic, salt, and pepper. Pour over salmon and marinate for 15 minutes.

Preheat grill to medium-high. Grill salmon, skin-side down, for 5-6 minutes per side, until cooked.

Garnish with lemon slices and fresh dill. Serve warm.

Mediterranean Sea Bass with Olives and Tomatoes

INGREDIENTS

- Sea Bass Fillets: 4 (6 oz each)
- Olive Oil: 2 tbsp
- Garlic: 2 cloves, minced
- Cherry Tomatoes: 1 cup, halved
- Kalamata Olives: 1/2 cup, pitted and halved
- Fresh Lemon Juice: 2 tbsp
- Fresh Parsley: 2 tbsp, chopped
- Salt and Pepper: To taste

Prep Time: 10 min

Cook Time: 20 min

Serves: 4

Nutritional Info (per serving):

Calories: 310/Protein: 30g/Carbs:5g/Fats: 18g/Fiber: 2g/Sodium: 450mg

DIRECTIONS

Heat olive oil in a skillet over medium heat. Add garlic and sauté for 1 minute.

Add sea bass fillets to the skillet, skin-side down. Cook for 4-5 minutes per side, until cooked through.

Add cherry tomatoes and olives to the skillet. Cook for 2-3 minutes until tomatoes soften.

Drizzle with lemon juice, sprinkle with parsley, and season with salt and pepper. Serve warm.

Shrimp and Feta Stuffed Tomatoes

INGREDIENTS

- Large Tomatoes: 4
- Shrimp: 1/2 lb, chopped
- Feta Cheese: 1/2 cup, crumbled
- Olive Oil: 2 tbsp
- Garlic: 2 cloves, minced
- Fresh Dill or Parsley: 2 tbsp, chopped
- Lemon Juice: 1 tbsp
- Salt and Pepper: To taste

 Prep Time: 15 min

 Cook Time: 20 min

 Serves: 4

Nutritional Info (per serving):

Calories: 200/Protein: 15g/Carbs: 10g/Fats: 12g/Fiber: 3g/Sodium: 400mg

DIRECTIONS

Preheat oven to 375°F (190°C). Hollow out the tomatoes.

Sauté garlic in olive oil, add shrimp and cook until pink. Mix with feta, herbs, lemon juice, salt, and pepper. Fill tomatoes with the shrimp mixture. Bake for 15 minutes.

Serve warm, garnished with extra herbs if desired.

Baked Cod with Crispy Garlic and Chorizo Crumbs

INGREDIENTS

- Cod Fillets: 4 (6 oz each)
- Chorizo: 1/4 cup, chopped
- Garlic: 3 cloves, minced
- Bread Crumbs: 1/2 cup
- Olive Oil: 2 tbsp
- Fresh Parsley: 2 tbsp, chopped
- Lemon Zest: 1 tsp
- Salt and Pepper: To taste
- Lemon Wedges: For serving

 Prep Time: 10 min

 Cook Time: 20 min

 Serves: 4

Nutritional Info (per serving):

Calories: 320/Protein: 30g/Carbs:12g/Fats: 18g/Fiber: 1g/Sodium: 600mg

DIRECTIONS

Preheat to 400°F (200°C).

Sauté chorizo in 1 tbsp olive oil until crispy. Add garlic and bread crumbs and cook until golden. Mix in parsley and lemon zest.

Place cod on a baking sheet, drizzle with olive oil, and season with salt and pepper. Top with crumb mixture.

Bake for 12-15 minutes until the cod is cooked through.

Serve with lemon wedges.

Moroccan Spiced Sardines

INGREDIENTS

- Sardines: 12, cleaned
- Olive Oil: 3 tbsp
- Garlic: 3 cloves, minced
- Cumin: 1 tsp
- Coriander: 1 tsp
- Paprika: 1 tsp
- Cinnamon: 1/4 tsp
- Fresh Cilantro: 1/4 cup, chopped
- Lemon Juice: 2 tbsp
- Salt and Pepper: To taste
- Lemon Wedges: For serving

Prep Time: 15 min

Cook Time: 10 min

Serves: 4

Nutritional Info (per serving):

Calories: 280/Protein: 25g/Carbs: 2g/Fats: 19g/Fiber: 1g/Sodium: 200mg

DIRECTIONS

Mix olive oil, garlic, cumin, coriander, paprika, cinnamon, cilantro, lemon juice, salt, and pepper.
Coat sardines with the marinade and let sit for 15 minutes.
Grill or pan-fry sardines for 3-4 minutes per side until cooked.
Serve with lemon wedges.

Herb-Crusted Tilapia with Lemon Butter

INGREDIENTS

- Tilapia Fillets: 4 (6 oz each)
- Olive Oil: 2 tbsp
- Fresh Parsley, Basil, Thyme: 1/4 cup each, chopped
- Garlic: 2 cloves, minced
- Bread Crumbs: 1/2 cup
- Lemon Zest: 1 tsp
- Salt and Pepper: To taste

Prep Time: 10 min

Cook Time: 15 min

Serves: 4

Nutritional Info (per serving):

Calories: 280/Protein: 30g/Carbs:10g/Fats: 14g/Fiber: 1g/Sodium: 300mg

DIRECTIONS

Preheat to 400°F (200°C). Mix bread crumbs, herbs, garlic, lemon zest, salt, pepper, and olive oil.
Press herb mixture onto tilapia fillets. Bake for 12-15 minutes.
Melt butter and stir in lemon juice.
Drizzle lemon butter over the tilapia and serve.

Pan-Seared Scallops with Sun-Dried Tomato Pesto

INGREDIENTS

For the Scallops:

- Sea Scallops: 1 lb (about 16)
- Olive Oil: 2 tbsp
- Salt and Pepper: To taste

For the Pesto:

- Sun-Dried Tomatoes: 1/2 cup, drained
- Fresh Basil: 1/2 cup
- Pine Nuts: 1/4 cup, toasted
- Parmesan Cheese: 1/4 cup, grated
- Garlic: 2 cloves
- Olive Oil: 1/4 cup
- Lemon Juice: 1 tbsp
- Salt and Pepper: To taste

 Prep Time: 15 min

 Cook Time: 10 min

 Serves: 4

Nutritional Info (per serving):

Calories: 350/Protein: 22g/Carbs: 6g/Fats: 26g/Fiber: 2g/Sodium: 450mg

DIRECTIONS

Blend sun-dried tomatoes, basil, pine nuts, Parmesan, garlic, olive oil, and lemon juice until smooth. Season with salt and pepper.

Pat scallops dry, season with salt and pepper, and sear in hot olive oil for 2-3 minutes per side until golden and cooked.

Serve scallops over the pesto and garnish with fresh basil and lemon wedges.

Clams in White Wine Sauce with Fresh Herbs

INGREDIENTS

- Fresh Clams: 2 lbs, scrubbed
- Olive Oil: 2 tbsp
- Garlic: 4 cloves, minced
- Shallot: 1 chopped
- White Wine: 1 cup
- Broth: 1/2 cup (chicken or vegetable)
- Fresh Parsley: 1/4 cup, chopped
- Fresh Basil: 2 tbsp, chopped
- Fresh Thyme: 1 tbsp, chopped
- Lemon Juice: 1 tbsp
- Salt and Pepper: To taste

 Prep Time: 10 min

 Cook Time: 15 min

 Serves: 4

Nutritional Info (per serving):

Calories: 250/Protein: 22g/Carbs:8g/Fats: 10g/Fiber: 1g/Sodium: 600mg

DIRECTIONS

Heat olive oil in a skillet; sauté garlic and shallot for 2-3 minutes.

Add white wine and broth, simmer, and add the clams; cover and cook for 5-7 minutes until they open.

Stir in parsley, basil, thyme, and lemon juice. Season with salt and pepper.

Serve clams in broth with crusty bread.

Grilled Octopus with Oregano and Lemon

INGREDIENTS

- Octopus: 2 lbs, cleaned
- Olive Oil: 1/4 cup
- Lemon Juice: 2 tbsp
- Lemon Zest: 1 tsp
- Fresh Oregano: 2 tbsp, chopped
- Garlic: 2 cloves, minced
- Salt and Pepper: To taste
- Lemon Wedges: For serving

 Prep Time: 20 min

 Cook Time: 60 min

 Serves: 4

Nutritional Info (per serving):

Calories: 250/Protein: 26g/Carbs: 2g/Fats: 14g/Fiber: 0g/Sodium: 300mg

DIRECTIONS

Boil the octopus in water for 45 minutes until tender. Drain and cool then cut into pieces.

Mix olive oil, lemon juice, zest, oregano, garlic, salt, and pepper. Toss the octopus in the marinade and let it sit for 15 minutes.

Preheat grill to medium-high. Grill octopus for 3-4 minutes per side until charred. Serve with lemon wedges and garnish with fresh oregano.

Swordfish Steaks with Capers and Roasted Peppers

INGREDIENTS

- Swordfish Steaks: 4 (6 oz each)
- Olive Oil: 3 tbsp
- Garlic: 2 cloves, minced
- Capers: 2 tbsp
- Roasted Red Peppers: 1 cup, sliced
- Lemon Juice: 2 tbsp
- Fresh Parsley: 2 tbsp, chopped
- Salt and Pepper: To taste

 Prep Time: 15 min

 Cook Time: 15 min

 Serves: 4

Nutritional Info (per serving):

Calories: 320/Protein: 30g/Carbs:5g/Fats: 20g/Fiber: 1g/Sodium: 400mg

DIRECTIONS

Season swordfish with salt and pepper. Heat 2 tbsp olive oil in a skillet over medium-high heat. Cook swordfish for 4-5 minutes per side until golden and cooked through. Remove and set aside.

In the same skillet, add 1 tbsp olive oil. Sauté garlic for 1 minute, then add capers and roasted peppers. Cook for 2-3 minutes.

Return swordfish to skillet, drizzle with lemon juice, and cook for 1-2 more minutes. Garnish with parsley.

Anchovy and Cherry Tomato Pasta

INGREDIENTS

- Spaghetti: 12 oz
- Olive Oil: 3 tbsp
- Anchovy Fillets: 8 chopped
- Garlic: 4 cloves, minced
- Cherry Tomatoes: 2 cups, halved
- Red Pepper Flakes: 1/2 tsp (optional)
- Fresh Basil: 1/4 cup, chopped
- Fresh Parsley: 1/4 cup, chopped
- Lemon Zest: 1 tsp
- Salt and Pepper: To taste

 Prep Time: 10 min

 Cook Time: 15 min

 Serves: 4

Nutritional Info (per serving):

Calories: 380/Protein: 12g/Carbs: 54g/Fats: 14g/Fiber: 3g/Sodium: 500mg

DIRECTIONS

Cook spaghetti in salted water until al dente. Reserve 1/2 cup pasta water, then drain.

Heat olive oil in a skillet. Cook the anchovies until dissolved. Add garlic and red pepper flakes and sauté for 1 minute. Add tomatoes and cook until softened.

Toss pasta with the sauce, adding reserved pasta water if needed. Stir in basil, parsley, and lemon zest. Season with salt and pepper.

Garnish with fresh herbs.

Mediterranean Baked Salmon with Feta and Spinach

INGREDIENTS

- Salmon Fillets: 4 (6 oz each)
- Fresh Spinach: 4 cups, chopped
- Feta Cheese: 1/2 cup, crumbled
- Olive Oil: 2 tbsp
- Garlic: 3 cloves, minced
- Lemon Juice: 2 tbsp
- Salt and Pepper: To taste

 Prep Time: 10 min

 Cook Time: 20 min

 Serves: 4

Nutritional Info (per serving):

Calories: 380/Protein: 35g/Carbs:4g/Fats: 24g/Fiber: 1g/Sodium: 450mg

DIRECTIONS

Preheat to 375°F (190°C).

Sauté garlic in 1 tbsp olive oil until fragrant. Add spinach and cook until wilted.

Stir in feta and lemon juice, season with salt and pepper.

Place salmon on a baking sheet, season, and top with the spinach mixture.

Drizzle with remaining olive oil.

Bake for 15-20 minutes, until salmon is cooked through.

Seared Tuna Steaks with Olive Tapenade

INGREDIENTS

For the Tuna Steaks:

- Tuna Steaks: 4 (6 oz each)
- Olive Oil: 2 tbsp
- Salt and Pepper: To taste

For the Olive Tapenade:

- Kalamata Olives: 1 cup, pitted
- Capers: 2 tbsp
- Garlic: 2 cloves, minced
- Fresh Parsley: 1/4 cup, chopped
- Lemon Juice: 1 tbsp
- Olive Oil: 2 tbsp

 Prep Time: 10 min

Cook Time: 10 min

 Serves: 4

Nutritional Info (per serving):

Calories: 350/Protein: 35g/Carbs: 4g/Fats: 22g/Fiber: 2g/Sodium: 600mg

DIRECTIONS

Pulse olives, capers, garlic, parsley, lemon juice, and olive oil in a food processor until finely chopped. Set aside.

Season tuna with salt and pepper. Heat olive oil in a skillet over medium-high heat. Sear tuna for 2-3 minutes per side for medium-rare.

Top the tuna with olive tapenade and serve with lemon wedges.

Baked Mackerel with Lemon and Thyme

INGREDIENTS

- Mackerel Fillets: 4 (6 oz each)
- Olive Oil: 2 tbsp
- Lemon Juice: 2 tbsp
- Fresh Thyme: 2 tbsp, chopped
- Garlic: 2 cloves, minced
- Salt and Pepper: To taste

 Prep Time: 10 min

 Cook Time: 20 min

 Serves: 4

Nutritional Info (per serving):

Calories: 320/Protein: 28g/Carbs:2g/Fats: 20g/Fiber: 0g/Sodium: 150mg

DIRECTIONS

Preheat to 375°F (190°C).

Place fillets in a baking dish. Drizzle with olive oil and lemon juice, then sprinkle with thyme, garlic, salt, and pepper.

Bake for 15-20 minutes until the fish flakes easily with a fork.

Garnish with lemon slices

Fish Tagine with Preserved Lemon and Olives

INGREDIENTS

- White Fish Fillets: 4 (6 oz each)
- Olive Oil: 3 tbsp
- Onion: 1, sliced
- Garlic: 3 cloves, minced
- Preserved Lemon: 1, sliced
- Green Olives: 1/2 cup
- Cherry Tomatoes: 1 cup
- Ground Cumin: 1 tsp
- Fresh Cilantro and Parsley: 1/4 cup each, chopped
- Lemon Juice: 2 tbsp
- Salt and Pepper: To taste

 Prep Time: 15 min

 Cook Time: 30 min

 Serves: 4

Nutritional Info (per serving):

Calories: 350/Protein: 30g/Carbs: 10g/Fats: 20g/Fiber: 4g/Sodium: 600mg

DIRECTIONS

Sauté onion in olive oil until soft. Add garlic and cumin, and cook briefly.
Stir in lemon, olives, tomatoes. Season fish with salt and pepper and place on top.
Add lemon juice, cover, and cook for 20-25 minutes.
Garnish with cilantro and parsley.

Calamari Stuffed with Rice and Herbs

INGREDIENTS

- Calamari Tubes: 8
- Cooked Rice: 1 cup
- Olive Oil: 2 tbsp
- Onion: 1 small, chopped
- Garlic: 2 cloves, minced
- Fresh Parsley: 1/4 cup, chopped
- Fresh Dill: 1/4 cup, chopped
- Pine Nuts: 1/4 cup, toasted
- Lemon Juice: 2 tbsp
- Salt and Pepper: To taste

 Prep Time: 20 min

 Cook Time: 25 min

 Serves: 4

Nutritional Info (per serving):

Calories: 280/Protein: 22g/Carbs:20g/Fats: 12g/Fiber: 2g/Sodium: 300mg

DIRECTIONS

Sauté onion in 1 tbsp olive oil until soft. Add garlic and cook briefly. Mix with rice, parsley, dill, pine nuts, lemon juice, salt, and pepper.
Fill calamari tubes with rice mixture and secure them with toothpicks.
Heat the remaining oil in a skillet. Cook stuffed calamari for 8-10 minutes, turning occasionally.
Serve with lemon wedges and a salad.

Saffron-Infused Seafood Stew

INGREDIENTS

- Olive Oil: 2 tbsp
- Onion: 1, chopped
- Garlic: 3 cloves, minced
- Fennel: 1 bulb, sliced
- Carrot: 1, sliced
- Saffron: 1/2 tsp, steeped in warm water
- White Wine: 1/2 cup
- Fish Stock: 4 cups
- Diced Tomatoes: 1 can (14 oz)
- Mixed Seafood: 1 lb (shrimp, mussels, fish)
- Salt and Pepper: To taste
- Parsley: 1/4 cup, chopped

 Prep Time: 15 min

 Cook Time: 30 min

Serves: 4

Nutritional Info (per serving):

Calories: 320/Protein: 30g/Carbs: 12g/Fats: 12g/Fiber: 3g/Sodium: 600mg

DIRECTIONS

Cook onion, garlic, fennel, and carrot in olive oil until soft.
Add saffron, wine, stock, and tomatoes. Simmer for 15 minutes. Add seafood and cook for 5-7 minutes. Season.
Garnish with parsley.

Spicy Mussels in Tomato and White Wine Sauce

INGREDIENTS

- Mussels: 2 lbs, cleaned
- Olive Oil: 2 tbsp
- Garlic: 4 cloves, minced
- Red Pepper Flakes: 1/2 tsp
- White Wine: 1 cup
- Diced Tomatoes: 1 can (14 oz)
- Fresh Parsley: 1/4 cup, chopped
- Fresh Basil: 1/4 cup, chopped
- Salt and Pepper: To taste

 Prep Time: 10 min

 Cook Time: 15 min

Serves: 4

Nutritional Info (per serving):

Calories: 250/Protein: 20g/Carbs:8g/Fats: 12g/Fiber: 2g/Sodium: 600mg

DIRECTIONS

Heat olive oil, add garlic and red pepper flakes, and sauté for 1 minute. Pour in white wine and tomatoes, and simmer.
Add mussels, cover, and cook for 5-7 minutes until mussels open.
Stir in parsley and basil, season with salt and pepper. Serve hot.

Chapter 7
Poultry Recipes

Greek Lemon Chicken with Potatoes

INGREDIENTS

- Chicken Thighs: 4 (bone-in, skin-on)
- Potatoes: 4 medium, wedged
- Olive Oil: 3 tbsp
- Lemon Juice: 1/4 cup
- Garlic: 4 cloves, minced
- Oregano: 2 tsp
- Salt and Pepper: To taste
- Chicken Broth: 1/2 cup

 Prep Time: 15 min

 Cook Time: 1 hour

 Serves: 4

Nutritional Info (per serving):

Calories: 450/Protein: 28g/Carbs: 30g/Fats: 23g/Fiber: 4g/Sodium: 400mg

DIRECTIONS

Preheat to 400°F (200°C).
Toss chicken and potatoes in olive oil, lemon juice, garlic, oregano, salt, and pepper.
Place in a baking dish, add broth, and bake for 45-60 minutes until chicken is golden and potatoes are tender.
Serve hot with your favorite sides.

Moroccan Chicken Tagine with Apricots and Almonds

INGREDIENTS

- Chicken Thighs: 4
- Olive Oil: 2 tbsp
- Onion: 1, chopped
- Garlic: 3 cloves, minced
- Ground Cumin: 1 tsp
- Ground Coriander: 1 tsp
- Ground Cinnamon: 1/2 tsp
- Chicken Broth: 1 cup
- Dried Apricots: 1/2 cup
- Almonds: 1/4 cup, toasted
- Honey: 1 tbsp
- Fresh Cilantro: 1/4 cup, chopped
- Salt and Pepper: To taste

 Prep Time: 15 min

 Cook Time: 1 hour

 Serves: 4

Nutritional Info (per serving):

Calories: 450/Protein: 28g/Carbs:25g/Fats: 26g/Fiber: 4g/Sodium: 400mg

DIRECTIONS

Heat oil, cook onion, garlic, and spices until fragrant.
Add and brown chicken thighs.
Add broth, apricots, and honey. Cover and simmer for 45-60 minutes.
Stir in almonds and cilantro before serving.

Mediterranean Stuffed Chicken with Feta and Spinach

INGREDIENTS

- Chicken Breasts: 4, boneless
- Spinach: 2 cups, chopped
- Feta Cheese: 1/2 cup, crumbled
- Sun-Dried Tomatoes: 1/4 cup, chopped
- Olive Oil: 2 tbsp
- Garlic: 2 cloves, minced
- Lemon Juice: 2 tbsp
- Oregano: 1 tsp
- Salt and Pepper: To taste

 Prep Time: 15 min

 Cook Time: 30 min

 Serves: 4

Nutritional Info (per serving):

Calories: 320/Protein: 36g/Carbs: 4g/Fats: 18g/Fiber: 2g/Sodium: 450mg

DIRECTIONS

Sauté garlic in 1 tbsp olive oil, add spinach, cook until wilted. Mix in feta and sun-dried tomatoes.

Cut a pocket in each chicken breast, fill it with spinach mixture, and secure it with toothpicks.

Sear the stuffed chicken in the remaining olive oil for 2-3 minutes per side. Drizzle with lemon juice and sprinkle with oregano, salt, and pepper.

Bake at 375°F (190°C) for 20-25 minutes until cooked.

Spanish Chicken and Chorizo Paella

INGREDIENTS

- Chicken Thighs: 4, cut into pieces
- Chorizo: 4 oz, sliced
- Onion: 1, chopped
- Garlic: 3 cloves, minced
- Red Bell Pepper: 1 sliced
- Arborio Rice: 1 cup
- Chicken Broth: 3 cups
- Diced Tomatoes: 1 cup
- Olive Oil: 2 tbsp
- Smoked Paprika: 1 tsp
- Saffron: A pinch (optional)
- Frozen Peas: 1/2 cup
- Salt, Pepper, Parsley, Lemon: To taste

 Prep Time: 15 min

 Cook Time: 40 min

 Serves: 4

Nutritional Info (per serving):

Calories: 450/Protein: 30g/Carbs:40g/Fats: 18g/Fiber: 4g/Sodium: 800mg

DIRECTIONS

Brown chicken and chorizo in olive oil. Set aside.

Sauté onion, garlic, and bell pepper. Add tomatoes, paprika, and saffron.

Stir in rice and broth. Add chicken and chorizo back. Simmer for 20 minutes. Add peas for the last 5 minutes.

Garnish with parsley and lemon.

Italian Chicken Cacciatore
with Olives and Tomatoes

INGREDIENTS

- Chicken Thighs: 4, skinless
- Olive Oil: 2 tbsp
- Onion: 1 chopped
- Garlic: 3 cloves, minced
- Red Bell Pepper: 1, sliced
- Mushrooms: 1 cup, sliced
- Diced Tomatoes: 1 can (14.5 oz)
- Black Olives: 1/2 cup
- White Wine: 1/2 cup
- Chicken Broth: 1/2 cup
- Rosemary & Thyme: 1 tsp each, chopped
- Salt and Pepper: To taste
- Fresh Parsley: For garnish

Prep Time: 15 min   Cook Time: 45 min   Serves: 4

Nutritional Info (per serving):

Calories: 350/Protein: 28g/Carbs: 10g/Fats: 22g/Fiber: 3g/Sodium: 800mg

DIRECTIONS

Season and brown chicken in olive oil, 5 minutes per side. Set aside.
In the same skillet, cook onion, garlic, bell pepper, and mushrooms until soft.
Stir in wine, tomatoes, broth, rosemary, and thyme. Simmer.
Return chicken and add olives. Cover and simmer 30 minutes.
Garnish with parsley.

Chicken Souvlaki with Cucumber-Yogurt Sauce

INGREDIENTS

For the Souvlaki:
- Chicken Breast: 1 lb, cubed
- Olive Oil: 2 tbsp
- Lemon Juice: 2 tbsp
- Garlic: 3 cloves, minced
- Oregano: 1 tsp
- Salt and Pepper: To taste

For the Sauce:
- Greek Yogurt: 1 cup
- Cucumber: 1/2, grated
- Garlic: 1 clove, minced
- Dill: 2 tbsp, chopped
- Lemon Juice: 1 tbsp
- Olive Oil: 1 tbsp
- Salt and Pepper: To taste

Prep Time: 20 min   Cook Time: 15 min   Serves: 4

Nutritional Info (per serving):

Calories: 320/Protein: 32g/Carbs:8g/Fats: 18g/Fiber: 1g/Sodium: 400mg

DIRECTIONS

Mix olive oil, lemon juice, garlic, oregano, salt, and pepper. Marinate chicken for 30 minutes (optional).
Combine yogurt, cucumber, garlic, dill, lemon juice, olive oil, salt, and pepper. Chill.
Thread chicken on skewers, grill, or cook in a skillet for 10-15 minutes until done.
Serve with the sauce and enjoy.

Chicken Marbella with Olives and Prunes

INGREDIENTS

- Chicken Thighs: 4, skinless
- Prunes: 1/2 cup, pitted
- Green Olives: 1/4 cup, pitted
- Capers: 2 tbsp
- Garlic: 4 cloves, minced
- Oregano: 1 tbsp
- Red Wine Vinegar: 1/4 cup
- Olive Oil: 2 tbsp
- Bay Leaves: 2
- Brown Sugar: 2 tbsp
- White Wine: 1/4 cup
- Salt and Pepper: To taste
- Fresh Parsley: For garnish

 Prep Time: 15 min   Cook Time: 1 hour   Serves: 4

Nutritional Info (per serving):

Calories: 380/Protein: 25g/Carbs: 18g/Fats: 22g/Fiber: 2g/Sodium: 600mg

DIRECTIONS

Combine prunes, olives, capers, garlic, oregano, vinegar, olive oil, bay leaves, salt, and pepper. Add chicken and marinate for 2 hours.
Preheat oven to 375°F. Place chicken and marinade in a baking dish. Sprinkle with brown sugar, add white wine, and bake for 50-60 minutes.
Garnish with parsley and serve.

Balsamic Glazed Chicken with Vegetables

INGREDIENTS

- Chicken Breasts: 4
- Balsamic Vinegar: 1/4 cup
- Olive Oil: 2 tbsp
- Garlic: 3 cloves, minced
- Honey: 1 tbsp
- Zucchini: 2, sliced
- Red Bell Pepper: 1, sliced
- Cherry Tomatoes: 1 cup, halved
- Red Onion: 1, sliced
- Salt, Pepper, Oregano, Thyme: To taste

 Prep Time: 10 min   Cook Time: 30 min   Serves: 4

Nutritional Info (per serving):

Calories: 380/Protein: 32g/Carbs:20g/Fats: 18g/Fiber: 4g/Sodium: 400mg

DIRECTIONS

Mix vinegar, oil, garlic, honey, oregano, salt, and pepper. Marinate chicken for 10 minutes.
Toss vegetables with olive oil, thyme, salt, and pepper. Roast at 400°F for 20-25 minutes.
Cook chicken in a skillet over medium heat, 6-7 minutes per side.
Serve chicken with vegetables.

Harissa Chicken Thighs
with Roasted Sweet Potatoes

INGREDIENTS

- Boneless, Skinless Chicken Thighs: 4
- Harissa Paste: 2 tbsp
- Olive Oil: 4 tbsp (divided)
- Sweet Potatoes: 2 large, cubed
- Cumin: 1 tsp (divided)
- Smoked Paprika: 1 tsp (divided)
- Salt and Pepper: To taste
- Fresh Herbs (Cilantro or Parsley): For garnish

Prep Time: 10 min

Cook Time: 35 min

Serves: 4

Nutritional Info (per serving):

Calories: 420/Protein: 25g/Carbs: 35g/Fats: 20g/Fiber: 6g/Sodium: 450mg

DIRECTIONS

Mix 2 tbsp olive oil, harissa, 1/2 tsp cumin, 1/2 tsp paprika, salt, and pepper. Coat chicken and marinate briefly.

Toss sweet potatoes with 2 tbsp olive oil, remaining cumin, paprika, salt, and pepper. Spread on a baking sheet.

Preheat the oven to 400°F (200°C). Roast the sweet potatoes for 30-35 minutes. Meanwhile, cook the chicken in a skillet over medium heat for 6-7 minutes per side.

Garnish chicken with cilantro or parsley and serve with roasted sweet potatoes.

Pomegranate and Walnut Chicken Stew

INGREDIENTS

- Chicken Thighs: 1 lb, cut into pieces
- Onion: 1 large, chopped
- Garlic: 2 cloves, minced
- Walnuts: 1 cup, ground
- Pomegranate Juice: 1 cup
- Chicken Broth: 1/2 cup
- Cinnamon: 1 tsp
- Turmeric: 1 tsp
- Cumin: 1/2 tsp
- Olive Oil: 2 tbsp
- Salt and Pepper: To taste
- Fresh Herbs and Pomegranate Seeds: For garnish

Prep Time: 10 min

Cook Time: 45 min

Serves: 4

Nutritional Info (per serving):

Calories: 420/Protein: 28g/Carbs:15g/Fats: 30g/Fiber: 3g/Sodium: 300mg

DIRECTIONS

Season chicken with salt and pepper. Brown in 1 tbsp olive oil over medium heat. Remove and set aside.

In the same skillet, sauté onions in remaining olive oil until golden. Add garlic and cook for 1 minute.

Add walnuts, spices, pomegranate juice, and chicken broth. Bring to a simmer, then add chicken. Cover and cook on low for 30 minutes.

Garnish with fresh herbs and pomegranate seeds. Serve with quinoa or couscous.

Sumac Chicken with Red Onion and Arugula Salad

INGREDIENTS

- Boneless, Skinless Chicken Breasts: 4
- Sumac: 2 tbsp
- Cumin: 1 tsp
- Garlic Powder: 1 tsp
- Olive Oil: 2 tbsp
- Salt and Pepper: To taste
- Arugula: 4 cups
- Red Onion: 1, thinly sliced
- Cherry Tomatoes: 1/2 cup, halved
- Walnuts: 1/4 cup, chopped
- Lemon Juice: 2 tbsp
- Olive Oil (for dressing): 2 tbsp

 Prep Time: 10 min

 Cook Time: 20 min

 Serves: 4

Nutritional Info (per serving):

Calories: 350/Protein: 30g/Carbs: 10g/Fats: 20g/Fiber: 3g/Sodium: 250mg

DIRECTIONS

Rub chicken with sumac, cumin, garlic powder, salt, and pepper.

Heat olive oil in a skillet over medium heat. Cook chicken for 6-7 minutes per side until done. Let rest, then slice.

Combine the arugula, red onion, cherry tomatoes, and walnuts in a bowl. Drizzle with lemon juice and olive oil and season with salt and pepper.

Top salad with sliced chicken and enjoy.

Grilled Chicken with Lemon, Garlic, and Oregano

INGREDIENTS

- Boneless, Skinless Chicken Breasts: 4
- Olive Oil: 1/4 cup
- Garlic: 3 cloves, minced
- Lemon Juice and Zest: Juice and zest of 1 lemon
- Fresh Oregano: 2 tbsp (or 1 tbsp dried)
- Salt and Pepper: To taste
- Lemon Wedges and Fresh Herbs: For garnish

 Prep Time: 10 min

 Cook Time: 15 min

 Serves: 4

Nutritional Info (per serving):

Calories: 300/Protein: 28g/Carbs:2g/Fats: 20g/Fiber: 0g/Sodium: 180mg

DIRECTIONS

Mix olive oil, garlic, lemon juice, zest, oregano, salt, and pepper. Coat chicken in the marinade and refrigerate for 30 minutes.

Preheat the grill to medium-high. Grill the chicken for 6-7 minutes per side until cooked through. Let it rest.

Garnish with lemon wedges and herbs. Pair with grilled veggies or a salad.

Mediterranean Chicken Orzo Soup

INGREDIENTS

- Chicken Breast: 1 lb, diced
- Olive Oil: 1 tbsp
- Onion: 1 small, diced
- Garlic: 2 cloves, minced
- Carrots: 2, diced
- Celery Stalks: 2 diced
- Dried Oregano: 1 tsp
- Dried Thyme: 1 tsp
- Chicken Broth: 6 cups
- Orzo Pasta: 1 cup
- Baby Spinach: 1 cup, chopped
- Lemon Juice: Juice of 1 lemon
- Salt and Pepper: To taste
- Fresh Parsley: For garnish

 Prep Time: 10 min

 Cook Time: 25 min

 Serves: 4

Nutritional Info (per serving):

Calories: 320/Protein: 28g/Carbs: 35g/Fats: 8g/Fiber: 4g/Sodium: 400mg

DIRECTIONS

Heat olive oil in a pot over medium heat. Cook diced chicken until browned, then set aside.

In the same pot, sauté onion, garlic, carrots, and celery for 5 minutes.

Add oregano, thyme, broth, and orzo. Simmer for 10-12 minutes until the orzo is tender. Return the chicken to the pot.

Stir in spinach and lemon juice. Season with salt and pepper. Garnish with parsley.

Garlic and Rosemary Roasted Chicken Thighs

INGREDIENTS

- Bone-In, Skin-On Chicken Thighs: 8
- Fresh Rosemary: 3 sprigs, chopped
- Garlic: 4 cloves, minced
- Olive Oil: 2 tbsp
- Lemon Juice: Juice of 1 lemon
- Salt and Pepper: To taste

 Prep Time: 10 min

 Cook Time: 35-40 min

 Serves: 4

Nutritional Info (per serving):

Calories: 380/Protein: 25g/Carbs:2g/Fats: 30g/Fiber: 0g/Sodium: 400mg

DIRECTIONS

Preheat to 400°F (200°C).

Mix olive oil, garlic, rosemary, lemon juice, salt, and pepper. Coat chicken thighs in the mixture.

Place thighs skin-side up on a baking sheet and roast for 35-40 minutes until crispy and cooked.

Rest for a few minutes before serving. Garnish with extra rosemary if desired.

Chicken Piccata with Capers and Lemon Butter Sauce

INGREDIENTS

- Chicken Breasts: 4, pounded thin
- Whole Wheat Flour: 1/4 cup
- Salt and Pepper: To taste
- Olive Oil: 2 tbsp
- Butter: 3 tbsp, divided
- White Wine (or Chicken Broth): 1/4 cup
- Chicken Broth: 1/2 cup
- Lemon Juice: 1/4 cup
- Capers: 1/4 cup, drained
- Parsley: 2 tbsp, chopped

 Prep Time: 10 min

 Cook Time: 20 min

Serves: 4

Nutritional Info (per serving):

Calories: 320/Protein: 28g/Carbs: 8g/Fats: 18g/Fiber: 1g/Sodium: 450mg

DIRECTIONS

Coat chicken in flour, salt, and pepper.

Heat oil and 1 tbsp butter in skillet; cook chicken 4-5 min per side. Set aside.

Add wine, broth, lemon juice, and capers to the skillet; simmer for 3-4 min. Stir in the remaining butter.

Return chicken to skillet and warm through. Garnish with parsley.

Chicken and Fig Skewers with Honey-Lemon Glaze

INGREDIENTS

- Chicken Breasts: 1 lb, cubed
- Figs: 8 fresh, halved
- Olive Oil: 2 tbsp
- Thyme: 1 tsp
- Cumin: 1 tsp
- Salt and Pepper: To taste
- Skewers
  Glaze:
- Honey: 2 tbsp
- Lemon Juice: 2 tbsp
- Lemon Zest: 1 tsp
- Olive Oil: 1 tbsp
- Coriander: 1/2 tsp

 Prep Time: 10 min

 Cook Time: 15 min

Serves: 4

Nutritional Info (per serving):

Calories: 290/Protein: 26g/Carbs:22g/Fats: 10g/Fiber: 3g/Sodium: 200mg

DIRECTIONS

Toss chicken with olive oil, thyme, cumin, salt, and pepper.

Thread chicken and figs onto skewers.

Mix honey, lemon juice, zest, olive oil, and coriander.

Cook on medium-high heat, 4-5 min per side, brushing with glaze.

Chapter 8
Meat Recipes

Spanish Pork Chops with Pimentón and Garlic

INGREDIENTS

- Pork Chops: 4 (1-inch thick)
- Olive Oil: 2 tbsp
- Garlic: 4 cloves, minced
- Pimentón (Smoked Paprika): 2 tsp
- Cumin: 1 tsp
- Oregano: 1 tsp
- Salt and Pepper: To taste
- Lemon Juice: Juice of 1 lemon
- Fresh Parsley: 2 tbsp, chopped (for garnish)

 Prep Time: 10 min

 Cook Time: 20 min

 Serves: 4

Nutritional Info (per serving):

Calories: 320/Protein: 28g/Carbs: 3g/Fats: 22g/Fiber: 1g/Sodium: 500mg

DIRECTIONS

Rub pork chops with olive oil, garlic, pimentón, cumin, oregano, salt, and pepper. Sear in a hot skillet, 4-5 min per side, until cooked through. Finish with lemon juice.
Garnish with parsley.

Italian Beef Osso Bucco with Gremolata

INGREDIENTS

- Beef Shanks: 4
- Olive Oil: 3 tbsp
- Onion: 1, diced
- Carrots: 2, diced
- Celery: 2 stalks, diced
- Garlic: 4 cloves, minced
- Tomato Paste: 2 tbsp
- White Wine: 1 cup
- Beef Broth: 2 cups
- Diced Tomatoes: 1 cup
- Bay Leaves: 2
- Thyme: 1 tsp
- Salt and Pepper: To taste
  Gremolata:
- Parsley: 1/4 cup, chopped
- Garlic: 1 clove, minced
- Lemon Zest: 1 lemon

 Prep Time: 15 min

 Cook Time: 2 hours

 Serves: 4

Nutritional Info (per serving):

Calories: 460/Protein: 36g/Carbs:12g/Fats: 28g/Fiber: 3g/Sodium: 480mg

DIRECTIONS

Season and sear shanks in olive oil. Remove and set aside.
Sauté onion, carrots, celery, and garlic. Add tomato paste.
Add wine, broth, tomatoes, bay leaves, and thyme. Return beef and simmer.
Cover the skillet and transfer to a preheated oven at 325°F (165°C) for 1.5-2 hours.
Mix parsley, garlic, and lemon zest.
Plate with gremolata.

Moroccan Lamb Tagine with Prunes and Almonds

INGREDIENTS

- Lamb Shoulder: 1 lb, cubed
- Olive Oil: 2 tbsp
- Onion: 1, diced
- Garlic: 3 cloves, minced
- Cumin, Cinnamon, Ginger: 1 tsp each
- Turmeric and coriander: 1/2 tsp each
- Broth: 2 cups
- Prunes: 1/2 cup
- Almonds: 1/4 cup
- Honey: 1 tbsp
- Cilantro: For garnish
- Salt and Pepper: To taste

Prep Time: 15 min   Cook Time: 1 hr 30 min   Serves: 4

Nutritional Info (per serving):

Calories: 450/Protein: 28g/Carbs: 25g/Fats: 28g/Fiber: 5g/Sodium: 300mg

DIRECTIONS

Brown lamb cubes in olive oil; set aside.
Sauté onion, garlic, and spices.
Return lamb, add broth, and simmer for 1 hour.
Stir in prunes, almonds, and honey. Cook 20-30 min until the lamb is tender.
Garnish with cilantro.

Provençal Beef Stew with Red Wine and Olives

INGREDIENTS

- Beef Chuck: 1 lb, cubed
- Olive Oil: 2 tbsp
- Onion: 1, diced
- Carrots: 2, sliced
- Celery: 2 stalks, sliced
- Garlic: 3 cloves, minced
- Red Wine: 1 cup
- Beef Broth: 2 cups
- Diced Tomatoes: 1 cup
- Tomato Paste: 2 tbsp
- Bay Leaves: 2
- Thyme & Rosemary: 1 tsp each
- Black Olives: 1/2 cup, halved
- Salt & Pepper: To taste
- Parsley: For garnish

Prep Time: 15 min   Cook Time: 2 hr 30 min   Serves: 4

Nutritional Info (per serving):

Calories: 420/Protein: 30g/Carbs:16g/Fats: 22g/Fiber: 4g/Sodium: 600mg

DIRECTIONS

Brown beef in olive oil, set aside.
Sauté onion, carrots, celery, garlic.
Add wine and stir to deglaze.
Add tomatoes, broth, beef, herbs, salt, pepper. Simmer covered for 2 hours.
Stir in olives and cook uncovered for 30 minutes. Garnish with parsley.

Mediterranean Herb-Crusted Rack of Lamb

INGREDIENTS

- Rack of Lamb: 1 (1.5 lbs)
- Olive Oil: 2 tbsp
- Garlic: 4 cloves, minced
- Rosemary, Thyme, Oregano: 2 tbsp each, chopped
- Dijon Mustard: 2 tbsp
- Lemon Zest: 1 tsp
- Salt and Pepper: To taste
- Panko Breadcrumbs: 1/2 cup (optional)

 Prep Time: 15 min   Cook Time: 25-30 min   Serves: 4

Nutritional Info (per serving):

Calories: 450/Protein: 28g/Carbs: 5g/Fats: 36g/Fiber: 1g/Sodium: 300mg

DIRECTIONS

Preheat your oven to 400°F (200°C).

Combine garlic, herbs, olive oil, mustard, lemon zest, salt, and pepper.

Pat the rack of lamb dry, coat with herb mixture, and sprinkle with panko if using.

Sear fat side down in a hot skillet for 2-3 min.

Transfer to oven and roast for 20-25 min for medium-rare.

Let rest for 10 min before slicing.

Turkish Beef Kebabs with Sumac Onions

INGREDIENTS

Beef Kebabs:

- Ground Beef: 1 lb
- Onion: 1 small, grated
- Garlic: 2 cloves, minced
- Parsley: 1/4 cup, chopped
- Cumin, Coriander, Paprika: 1 tsp each
- Sumac: 1/2 tsp
- Salt & Pepper: To taste
- Olive Oil: 2 tbsp (for brushing)

Sumac Onions:

- Red Onion: 1 large, sliced
- Sumac: 1 tbsp
- Parsley: 2 tbsp, chopped
- Lemon Juice: 2 tbsp
- Salt: To taste

 Prep Time: 20 min   Cook Time: 15 min   Serves: 4

Nutritional Info (per serving):

Calories: 350/Protein: 25g/Carbs:10g/Fats: 23g/Fiber: 2g/Sodium: 400mg

DIRECTIONS

Combine beef, onion, garlic, parsley, spices, salt, and pepper. Form into kebabs around skewers.

Brush kebabs with olive oil and grill for 4-5 min per side.

Toss sliced onions with sumac, parsley, lemon juice, and salt.

Top kebabs with sumac onions. Pair with a pita or salad.

Grilled Veal with Lemon and Herbs

INGREDIENTS

- Veal Cutlets: 4
- Olive Oil: 2 tbsp
- Lemon Juice: 2 tbsp
- Lemon Zest: 1 tsp
- Garlic: 3 cloves, minced
- Rosemary, Thyme, Oregano: 1 tbsp each, chopped
- Salt & Pepper: To taste
- Lemon Wedges & Parsley: For garnish

 Prep Time: 15 min

 Cook Time: 10 min

 Serves: 4

Nutritional Info (per serving):

Calories: 280/Protein: 24g/Carbs: 2g/Fats: 18g/Fiber: 1g/Sodium: 150mg

DIRECTIONS

Mix olive oil, lemon juice, zest, garlic, herbs, salt, and pepper. Coat veal and marinate for 15 min.
Preheat grill to medium-high. Grill veal 3-4 min per side.
Garnish with lemon wedges and parsley.

Sicilian Meatballs in Tomato and Capers Sauce

INGREDIENTS

Meatballs:

- Ground Beef or Veal: 1 lb
- Breadcrumbs: 1/4 cup
- Parmesan: 1/4 cup, grated
- Garlic: 2 cloves, minced
- Parsley: 2 tbsp, chopped
- Egg: 1, beaten
- Salt & Pepper: To taste
- Olive Oil: 2 tbsp (for frying)

Tomato and Capers Sauce:

- Olive Oil: 1 tbsp
- Onion: 1 small, diced
- Garlic: 2 cloves, minced
- Diced Tomatoes: 1 can (14.5 oz)
- Tomato Paste: 2 tbsp
- Capers: 2 tbsp, drained
- Fresh Basil: 2 tablespoons, chopped (optional)

 Prep Time: 20 min

 Cook Time: 30 min

 Serves: 4

Nutritional Info (per serving):

Calories: 350/Protein: 26g/Carbs:12g/Fats: 22g/Fiber: 3g/Sodium: 600mg

DIRECTIONS

Mix meatball ingredients and form into balls. Fry in olive oil until browned. Remove and set aside.
Sauté onion and garlic in olive oil. Add tomatoes, paste, and capers. Simmer for 15 minutes.
Add meatballs to the sauce and simmer for 15 minutes.
Garnish with fresh basil if desired.

Lebanese Kibbeh with Yogurt Sauce

INGREDIENTS

- Ground Lamb or Beef: 1 lb
- Bulgur: 1/2 cup, soaked
- Onion: 1 small, chopped
- Pine Nuts: 1/4 cup, toasted
- Allspice, Cinnamon: 1 tsp, 1/2 tsp
- Olive Oil: 2 tbsp
- Greek Yogurt: 1 cup
- Cucumber: 1, diced
- Garlic: 1 clove, minced
- Lemon Juice: 1 tbsp
- Mint: 2 tbsp, chopped
- Salt, Pepper: To taste

 Prep Time: 25 min

 Cook Time: 30 min

 Serves: 4

Nutritional Info (per serving):

Calories: 350/Protein: 25g/Carbs: 20g/Fats: 18g/Fiber: 4g/Sodium: 250mg

DIRECTIONS

Combine meat, bulgur, onion, nuts, spices, salt, and pepper. Form patties.
Fry in olive oil for 4-5 min per side until browned.
Mix yogurt, cucumber, garlic, lemon juice, mint, and salt.
Serve with yogurt sauce.

Cypriot Sausage and Halloumi Skewers

INGREDIENTS

- Sausage: 8 oz, sliced
- Halloumi: 8 oz, cubed
- Red Bell Pepper: 1 chopped
- Zucchini: 1 sliced
- Red Onion: 1, wedged
- Olive Oil: 2 tbsp
- Lemon Juice: 1 tbsp
- Oregano: 1 tsp
- Salt & Pepper: To taste
- Parsley: For garnish

 Prep Time: 15 min

 Cook Time: 10 min

 Serves: 4

Nutritional Info (per serving):

Calories: 350/Protein: 20g/Carbs:8g/Fats: 26g/Fiber: 2g/Sodium: 800mg

DIRECTIONS

Thread sausage, halloumi, and veggies onto skewers.
Brush with olive oil, lemon juice, oregano, salt, and pepper.
Cook on medium-high heat for 3-4 min per side.
Garnish with parsley.

Tuscan Roast Pork with Fennel and Rosemary

INGREDIENTS

- Pork Shoulder: 2 lbs, trimmed
- Fennel Bulb: 1, sliced
- Garlic: 4 cloves, minced
- Fresh Rosemary: 2 tbsp, chopped
- Olive Oil: 3 tbsp
- Lemon Juice: 2 tbsp
- Salt & Pepper: To taste
- White Wine (optional): 1/2 cup

 Prep Time: 15 min

 Cook Time: 1 hr 30 min

 Serves: 4

Nutritional Info (per serving):

Calories: 350/Protein: 33g/Carbs: 12g/Fats: 20g/Fiber: 4g/Sodium: 100mg

DIRECTIONS

Preheat Oven: 375°F (190°C).

Rub pork with olive oil, garlic, rosemary, lemon juice, salt, and pepper.

Place fennel slices in a roasting pan. Add pork on top.

Bake for 1 hr 30 min, basting with wine or pan juices if desired, until pork reaches 145°F (63°C) internally.

Let pork rest for 10 min before slicing. Serve with fennel and pan juices.

Venetian Liver and Onions with White Polenta

INGREDIENTS

Liver and Onions:

- Beef Liver: 1 lb, sliced
- Olive Oil: 2 tbsp
- Onions: 2 large, sliced
- Garlic: 3 cloves, minced
- White Wine: 1/2 cup (optional)
- Fresh Sage: 1 tbsp, chopped (or 1 tsp dried)
- Salt & Pepper: To taste

Polenta:

- Polenta: 1 cup
- Water or Broth: 4 cups
- Olive Oil: 2 tbsp
- Parmesan Cheese: 1/4 cup (optional)
- Salt: To taste

 Prep Time: 20 min

 Cook Time: 30 min

 Serves: 4

Nutritional Info (per serving):

Calories: 320/Protein: 30g/Carbs:28g/Fats: 14g/Fiber: 3g/Sodium: 250mg

DIRECTIONS

Boil water or broth and whisk in polenta. Simmer, stirring, for 25-30 min. Stir in olive oil, cheese, and salt.

Heat olive oil in a skillet. Cook onions until soft. Add liver and cook until browned. Add garlic and white wine. Simmer for 5 minutes. Stir in sage and season with salt and pepper. Spoon polenta onto plates and top with liver and onions.

Spanish Meatloaf with Chorizo and Manchego

INGREDIENTS

- Ground Beef: 1 lb
- Chorizo: 1/2 lb, crumbled
- Manchego Cheese: 1/2 cup shredded
- Onion: 1 small, chopped
- Garlic: 2 cloves, minced
- Egg: 1
- Breadcrumbs: 1/2 cup
- Tomato Paste: 2 tbsp
- Paprika: 1 tsp
- Cumin: 1/2 tsp
- Oregano: 1/2 tsp
- Salt and Pepper: To taste
- Olive Oil: 1 tbsp

Prep Time: 15 min

Cook Time: 50 min

Serves: 4

Nutritional Info (per serving):

Calories: 380/Protein: 30g/Carbs: 15g/Fats: 22g/Fiber: 2g/Sodium: 650mg

DIRECTIONS

Preheat Oven: 375°F (190°C).

Mix beef, chorizo, cheese, onion, garlic, egg, breadcrumbs, tomato paste, paprika, cumin, oregano, salt, and pepper.

Form into a loaf in a baking dish. Brush with olive oil.

Cook for 40-50 minutes, until internal temp reaches 160°F (71°C).

Let rest for 10 minutes before slicing.

Catalan Rabbit Stew with Snails and Herbs

INGREDIENTS

- Rabbit: 1.5 lbs, cut into pieces
- Snails: 1 cup (canned or pre-cooked)
- Olive Oil: 2 tbsp
- Onion: 1 large, chopped
- Garlic: 3 cloves, minced
- Tomato: 2 large, diced
- Red Bell Pepper: 1 chopped
- White Wine: 1/2 cup
- Chicken Broth: 1 cup
- Rosemary: 2 sprigs
- Thyme: 2 sprigs
- Paprika: 1 tsp
- Salt and Pepper: To taste
- Fresh Parsley: 2 tbsp, chopped (for garnish)

Prep Time: 20 min

Cook Time: 1 hour 30 min

Serves: 4

Nutritional Info (per serving):

Calories: 320/Protein: 32g/Carbs:12g/Fats: 15g/Fiber: 2g/Sodium: 500mg

DIRECTIONS

Heat olive oil in a pot, brown rabbit pieces, then set aside.

Cook onion, garlic, and bell pepper in the same pot until softened.

Stir in tomato and cook for 5 mins. Add white wine and scrape the pot.

Return the rabbit, add the broth, herbs, paprika, salt, and pepper, and simmer covered for 45 minutes.

Stir in snails and cook for 15 more minutes.

Remove rosemary and thyme. Garnish with fresh parsley before serving.

Chapter 9
Vegetable Recipes

Grilled Eggplant with Yogurt and Pomegranate Seeds

INGREDIENTS

- Eggplant: 2 medium, sliced into 1/2-inch rounds
- Olive Oil: 2 tbsp
- Salt: 1/2 tsp
- Black Pepper: 1/4 tsp
- Ground Cumin: 1/2 tsp
- Plain Greek Yogurt: 1 cup
- Pomegranate Seeds: 1/4 cup
- Fresh Mint: 2 tbsp, chopped (optional)
- Lemon Juice: 1 tbsp

Prep Time: 15 min

Cook Time: 10 min

Serves: 4

Nutritional Info (per serving):

Calories: 140/Protein: 5g/Carbs: 14g/Fats: 8g/Fiber: 6g/Sodium: 150mg

DIRECTIONS

Brush eggplant slices with olive oil and season with salt, pepper, and cumin.
Preheat grill to medium-high. Grill eggplant slices for 3-4 minutes per side until tender and charred.
Mix Greek yogurt with lemon juice. Season with salt to taste.
Arrange grilled eggplant on a platter. Drizzle with yogurt sauce and sprinkle with pomegranate seeds. Garnish with fresh mint if using.

Roasted Red Peppers Stuffed with Herbed Goat Cheese

INGREDIENTS

- Red Bell Peppers: 4 large
- Goat Cheese: 8 oz, softened
- Fresh Basil: 2 tbsp, chopped
- Fresh Parsley: 2 tbsp, chopped
- Fresh Thyme: 1 tsp, chopped
- Garlic: 2 cloves, minced
- Olive Oil: 2 tbsp
- Lemon Zest: 1 tsp
- Salt and Pepper: To taste
- Pine Nuts: 2 tbsp, toasted (optional)

Prep Time: 15 min

Cook Time: 20 min

Serves: 4

Nutritional Info (per serving):

Calories: 200/Protein: 7g/Carbs:10g/Fats: 15g/Fiber: 3g/Sodium: 200mg

DIRECTIONS

Preheat Oven: 375°F (190°C).
Cut tops off peppers and remove seeds.
Combine goat cheese, herbs, garlic, olive oil, lemon zest, salt, and pepper.
Fill peppers with cheese mixture and top with pine nuts if using.
Bake for 20 minutes until peppers are tender.

Moroccan Spiced Carrot Salad
with Orange and Mint

INGREDIENTS

- Carrots: 4 large, julienned
- Orange: 1 large, segmented (reserve juice)
- Fresh Mint: 2 tbsp, chopped
- Cilantro: 2 tbsp, chopped
- Olive Oil: 2 tbsp
- Lemon Juice: 1 tbsp
- Honey: 1 tsp
- Ground Cumin: 1 tsp
- Ground Cinnamon: 1/2 tsp
- Ground Coriander: 1/2 tsp
- Salt and Pepper: To taste
- Optional: 2 tbsp toasted almonds or pistachios

Prep Time: 15 min

Cook Time: 0 min

Serves: 4

Nutritional Info (per serving):

Calories: 120/Protein: 1g/Carbs: 15g/Fats: 7g/Fiber: 4g/Sodium: 150mg

DIRECTIONS

Whisk olive oil, lemon juice, honey, spices, salt, pepper, and orange juice.
Mix carrots, orange segments, mint, and cilantro in a bowl. Pour dressing over.
Garnish with nuts if desired. Serve immediately or chill.

Caramelized Fennel
and Orange Salad with Arugula

INGREDIENTS

- Fennel Bulbs: 2, thinly sliced
- Olive Oil: 2 tbsp
- Honey: 1 tsp
- Orange: 2, segmented (reserve juice)
- Arugula: 4 cups
- Red Onion: 1/4 small, sliced
- Walnuts: 1/4 cup, toasted
- Balsamic Vinegar: 1 tbsp
- Salt and Pepper: To taste
- Fresh Mint: 2 tbsp, chopped (optional)

Prep Time: 15 min

Cook Time: 15 min

Serves: 4

Nutritional Info (per serving):

Calories: 180/Protein: 3g/Carbs:17g/Fats: 12g/Fiber: 4g/Sodium: 120mg

DIRECTIONS

Sauté fennel in 1 tbsp olive oil for 10-12 min until caramelized. Drizzle with honey and cool slightly.
Mix arugula, orange segments, onion, walnuts, and mint in a bowl.
Whisk remaining olive oil, orange juice, balsamic vinegar, salt, and pepper.
Add fennel to the salad, toss with dressing, and serve.

Turkish Zucchini Fritters with Dill and Feta

INGREDIENTS

- Zucchini: 3 medium, grated
- Salt: 1/2 tsp
- Eggs: 2, beaten
- Feta Cheese: 1/2 cup, crumbled
- Fresh Dill: 1/4 cup, chopped
- Green Onions: 2, finely chopped
- Garlic: 2 cloves, minced
- All-Purpose Flour: 1/2 cup
- Baking Powder: 1 tsp
- Black Pepper: 1/4 tsp
- Olive Oil: 2-3 tbsp (for frying)

 Prep Time: 15 min   Cook Time: 20 min   Serves: 4

Nutritional Info (per serving):

Calories: 180/Protein: 7g/Carbs: 12g/Fats: 12g/Fiber: 2g/Sodium: 300mg

DIRECTIONS

Grate zucchini, sprinkle with salt, and let sit for 10 min. Squeeze out moisture.
Combine zucchini, eggs, feta, dill, onions, garlic, flour, baking powder, and pepper.
Heat oil in a skillet. Form patties and cook for 3-4 min per side until golden.
Drain on paper towels and serve warm with yogurt or salad.

Mediterranean Roasted Vegetable Medley with Herbs de Provence

INGREDIENTS

- Zucchini: 1 medium, sliced
- Eggplant: 1 small, cubed
- Red Bell Pepper: 1, chopped
- Yellow Bell Pepper: 1 chopped
- Cherry Tomatoes: 1 cup
- Red Onion: 1 small, sliced
- Olive Oil: 3 tablespoons
- Herbs de Provence: 1 tablespoon
- Garlic: 3 cloves, minced
- Salt: 1/2 teaspoon
- Black Pepper: 1/4 teaspoon
- Fresh Basil: 2 tablespoons, chopped (optional)

 Prep Time: 15 min   Cook Time: 30-35 min   Serves: 4

Nutritional Info (per serving):

Calories: 150/Protein: 2g/Carbs:14g/Fats: 10g/Fiber: 4g/Sodium: 200mg

DIRECTIONS

Preheat Oven: 400°F (200°C).
Toss all vegetables with olive oil, Herbs de Provence, garlic, salt, and pepper.
Spread on a baking sheet and roast for 30-35 min, stirring halfway.
Garnish with basil if desired. Serve warm.

Italian Braised Artichokes with Capers and Lemon

INGREDIENTS

- Artichokes: 4 medium, trimmed and halved
- Olive Oil: 3 tablespoons
- Garlic: 3 cloves, minced
- Lemon: 1, juiced and zested
- Capers: 2 tablespoons, drained
- Vegetable Broth: 1 cup
- White Wine (optional): 1/4 cup
- Fresh Parsley: 2 tablespoons, chopped
- Salt and Pepper: To taste

 Prep Time: 15 min

 Cook Time: 30 min

 Serves: 4

Nutritional Info (per serving):

Calories: 140/Protein: 3g/Carbs: 12g/Fats: 9g/Fiber: 6g/Sodium: 300mg

DIRECTIONS

Halve and trim artichokes and rub them with lemon juice.
Heat olive oil in a skillet, sauté garlic until fragrant.
Place the artichokes cut side down. Add broth, wine (if using), lemon zest, capers, salt, and pepper.
Cover and simmer for 25-30 min until tender, stirring occasionally.
Top with parsley and a squeeze of lemon juice.

Baked Ratatouille with Thyme and Basil

INGREDIENTS

- Eggplant: 1 medium, sliced
- Zucchini: 2 medium, sliced
- Yellow Squash: 1, sliced
- Red Bell Pepper: 1, sliced
- Tomatoes: 3 medium, sliced
- Onion: 1 large, sliced
- Garlic: 3 cloves, minced
- Olive Oil: 3 tbsp
- Fresh Thyme: 1 tsp, chopped
- Fresh Basil: 2 tbsp, chopped
- Salt and Pepper: To taste
- Optional: 1 cup tomato sauce for the base

 Prep Time: 20 min

 Cook Time: 45 mi

 Serves: 4

Nutritional Info (per serving):

Calories: 180/Protein: 3g/Carbs:22g/Fats: 9g/Fiber: 7g/Sodium: 150mg

DIRECTIONS

Preheat Oven: 375°F (190°C).
Spread tomato sauce (if using) in a baking dish. Arrange sliced vegetables in a spiral pattern. Sprinkle with garlic.
Drizzle with olive oil, sprinkle with thyme, salt, and pepper.
Cover with foil and bake for 30 min. Remove the foil and bake for an additional 15 minutes, or until the vegetables are tender and slightly caramelized.
Garnish with fresh basil.

Lebanese Spinach Pies (Fatayer)

INGREDIENTS

For the Dough:

- All-Purpose Flour: 2 cups
- Instant Yeast: 1 tsp
- Salt: 1/2 tsp
- Olive Oil: 2 tbsp
- Warm Water: 3/4 cup

For the Filling:

- Fresh Spinach: 4 cups, chopped
- Onion: 1 medium, finely chopped
- Sumac: 1 tbsp
- Lemon Juice: 2 tbsp
- Olive Oil: 2 tbsp
- Salt: 1/2 tsp
- Black Pepper: 1/4 tsp
- Pine Nuts: 2 tbsp (optional)

 Prep Time: 30 min

 Cook Time: 20 min

 Serves: 4

Nutritional Info (per serving):

Calories: 180/Protein: 4g/Carbs: 22g/Fats: 8g/Fiber: 3g/Sodium: 300mg

DIRECTIONS

Mix flour, yeast, and salt. Add olive oil and water, knead until smooth, and let rise for 1 hour.

Sauté onion in olive oil. Add spinach and cook until wilted. Stir in sumac, lemon juice, salt, pepper, and pine nuts. Let cool.

Preheat oven to 375°F (190°C). Divide dough into 12 portions, roll into circles, and fill with spinach mix. Fold into triangles and seal edges.

Place on a baking sheet and bake for 15-20 minutes until golden.

Tunisian Chakchouka with Eggs and Olives

INGREDIENTS

- Olive Oil: 2 tbsp
- Onion: 1 large, chopped
- Bell Peppers: 2, chopped
- Garlic: 3 cloves, minced
- Tomatoes: 4, chopped (or 1 can be diced)
- Tomato Paste: 2 tbsp
- Harissa: 1-2 tsp
- Cumin: 1 tsp
- Paprika: 1 tsp
- Salt and Pepper: To taste
- Eggs: 4
- Olives: 1/4 cup, sliced
- Fresh Parsley or Cilantro: Optional

 Prep Time: 15 min

 Cook Time: 25 min

 Serves: 4

Nutritional Info (per serving):

Calories: 220/Protein: 10g/Carbs:14g/Fats: 15g/Fiber: 4g/Sodium: 500mg

DIRECTIONS

Heat olive oil and sauté onion and bell peppers for 5 min.

Stir in garlic, cumin, paprika, harissa, salt, and pepper. Cook for 1-2 min.

Add tomatoes and tomato paste. Simmer 10-15 min.

Make four wells in the sauce and crack an egg into each well. Cover and cook for 5-7 minutes.

Top with olives and parsley.

Sautéed Swiss Chard with Pine Nuts and Raisins

INGREDIENTS

- Swiss Chard: 1 bunch (about 12 oz), stems removed, leaves chopped
- Olive Oil: 2 tablespoons
- Garlic: 3 cloves, minced
- Pine Nuts: 1/4 cup, toasted
- Raisins: 1/4 cup
- Red Pepper Flakes: 1/4 teaspoon (optional)
- Salt and Pepper: To taste
- Lemon Juice: 1 tablespoon (optional)

Prep Time: 10 min

Cook Time: 15 min

Serves: 4

Nutritional Info (per serving):

Calories: 130/Protein: 2g/Carbs: 10g/Fats: 10g/Fiber: 2g/Sodium: 150mg

DIRECTIONS

In a dry skillet, toast pine nuts until golden, then set aside.
Heat olive oil in the same skillet, sauté garlic for 1 minute.
Add Swiss chard and cook until wilted, about 5-7 minutes.
Stir in raisins, pine nuts, and optional red pepper flakes. Cook for 2 minutes.
Season with salt, pepper, and optional lemon juice.

Egyptian Lentils and Rice with Fried Onions (Mujadara)

INGREDIENTS

- Brown or Green Lentils: 1 cup dried
- Rice: 1 cup, long-grain or basmati
- Olive Oil: 4 tablespoons, divided
- Onions: 2 large, thinly sliced
- Garlic: 2 cloves, minced
- Ground Cumin: 1 teaspoon
- Ground Coriander: 1 teaspoon
- Salt: 1 teaspoon
- Black Pepper: 1/2 teaspoon
- Water or Vegetable Broth: 3 cups
- Fresh Parsley: 2 tablespoons, chopped (for garnish)

Prep Time: 15 min

Cook Time: 45 min

Serves: 4

Nutritional Info (per serving):

Calories: 350/Protein: 10g/Carbs:50g/Fats: 12g/Fiber: 10g/Sodium: 400mg

DIRECTIONS

Simmer lentils in 2 cups of water for 15 min until tender. Drain and set aside.
Heat 2 tbsp olive oil in a skillet. Add rice, cooked lentils, cumin, coriander, salt, pepper, and 3 cups of water or broth. Simmer covered for 20-25 min until liquid is absorbed.
In a separate skillet, heat the remaining olive oil and fry the onions until golden brown, about 15-20 minutes.
Fluff rice and lentils, top with fried onions, and garnish with parsley. Serve warm.

Grilled Portobello Mushrooms
with Balsamic Reduction

INGREDIENTS

- Portobello Mushrooms: 4 large caps, stems removed
- Olive Oil: 3 tablespoons
- Balsamic Vinegar: 1/2 cup
- Garlic: 2 cloves, minced
- Fresh Thyme: 1 teaspoon, chopped (optional)
- Salt and Pepper: To taste
- Fresh Basil or Parsley: 2 tablespoons, chopped (for garnish)

 Prep Time: 10 min

 Cook Time: 20 min

 Serves: 4

Nutritional Info (per serving):

Calories: 130/Protein: 3g/Carbs: 10g/Fats: 9g/Fiber: 2g/Sodium: 100mg

DIRECTIONS

Simmer balsamic vinegar in a small saucepan until reduced by half, 10-15 min.
Brush mushrooms with olive oil and season with garlic, salt, pepper, and thyme. Marinate for 10 min.
Preheat the grill to medium heat. Grill mushrooms 4-5 min per side until tender.
Drizzle with balsamic reduction and garnish with basil or parsley.

Caponata: Sicilian Eggplant Stew
with Capers and Vinegar

INGREDIENTS

- Eggplant: 1 large, diced
- Olive Oil: 1/4 cup
- Onion: 1, chopped
- Celery Stalks: 2, chopped
- Garlic: 3 cloves, minced
- Tomatoes: 2, diced (or 1 can diced)
- Green Olives: 1/4 cup, sliced
- Capers: 2 tablespoons
- Red Wine Vinegar: 2 tablespoons
- Salt and Pepper: To taste
- Optional: 1 teaspoon sugar, 2 tablespoons pine nuts, fresh basil, or parsley for garnish

 Prep Time: 15 min

 Cook Time: 40 min

 Serves: 4

Nutritional Info (per serving):

Calories: 200/Protein: 3g/Carbs:15g/Fats: 14g/Fiber: 7g/Sodium: 350mg

DIRECTIONS

Salt diced eggplant, let it sit for 15 min, rinse it, and pat dry.
Heat olive oil, sauté onion and celery for 5 min, and add garlic.
Stir in eggplant and cook until soft. Add tomatoes, olives, capers, vinegar, and optional sugar.
Simmer 20-25 min until thickened.
Garnish with pine nuts and herbs if desired.

Greek Fava with Caramelized Onions and Capers

INGREDIENTS

- Yellow Split Peas (Fava): 1 cup
- Water: 4 cups
- Olive Oil: 3 tablespoons, divided
- Onions: 2 medium, thinly sliced
- Garlic: 2 cloves, minced
- Lemon Juice: 2 tablespoons
- Capers: 2 tablespoons, drained
- Fresh Thyme or Oregano: 1 teaspoon, chopped (optional)
- Salt and Pepper: To taste
- Fresh Parsley: 2 tablespoons, chopped (for garnish)

 Prep Time: 10 min
 Cook Time: 45 min
 Serves: 4

Nutritional Info (per serving):

Calories: 210/Protein: 8g/Carbs: 32g/Fats: 7g/Fiber: 10g/Sodium: 300mg

DIRECTIONS

Rinse split peas and cook with 4 cups of water for 40 min until soft. Mash and stir in 1 tbsp olive oil, lemon juice, salt, and pepper. Set aside.

Heat 2 tbsp olive oil in a skillet. Cook the onions until golden, about 15-20 minutes. Add the garlic in the last 2 minutes.

Spread mashed fava on a dish, top with caramelized onions, capers, and optional herbs, and garnish with parsley.

Provençal Tian of Zucchini, Tomato, and Potatoes

INGREDIENTS

- Zucchini: 2 medium, thinly sliced
- Tomatoes: 2 medium, thinly sliced
- Potatoes: 2 medium, thinly sliced
- Onion: 1 medium, thinly sliced
- Garlic: 2 cloves, minced
- Olive Oil: 3 tablespoons
- Fresh Thyme: 1 teaspoon, chopped
- Fresh Rosemary: 1 teaspoon, chopped (optional)
- Salt and Pepper: To taste
- Parmesan Cheese: 1/4 cup, grated (optional)

 Prep Time: 20 min
 Cook Time: 45 min
 Serves: 4

Nutritional Info (per serving):

Calories: 180/Protein: 4g/Carbs:20g/Fats: 10g/Fiber: 3g/Sodium: 150mg

DIRECTIONS

Preheat Oven: 375°F (190°C).

Sliced vegetables should be arranged in alternating layers in a baking dish.

Sprinkle with garlic, thyme, rosemary, salt, and pepper.

Drizzle with olive oil.

Cover with foil and bake for 30 min. Remove the foil, add Parmesan if used, and bake for 15 minutes more.

Cool slightly before serving.

Chapter 10
Desserts

Greek Honey and Walnut Baklava

INGREDIENTS

- Phyllo Dough: 8 sheets, thawed
- Walnuts: 1 cup, finely chopped
- Cinnamon: 1 teaspoon
- Butter: 1/4 cup, melted
- Honey: 1/2 cup
- Water: 1/4 cup
- Sugar: 2 tablespoons
- Lemon Juice: 1 teaspoon
- Vanilla Extract: 1/2 teaspoon

Prep Time: 20 min

Cook Time: 30 min

Serves: 4

Nutritional Info (per serving):

Calories: 350/Protein: 5g/Carbs: 38g/Fats: 20g/Fiber: 2g/Sodium: 150mg

DIRECTIONS

Preheat Oven: 350°F (175°C).
Mix walnuts and cinnamon.
Layer 2 sheets of phyllo in a buttered dish, brushing each with butter.
Sprinkle with a nut mixture. Repeat layers, ending with phyllo. Cut into shapes.
Bake 25-30 min until golden.
Simmer honey, water, sugar, lemon juice, and vanilla for 10 minutes.
Pour over baked baklava. Let sit for 4 hours or overnight.

Italian Lemon Ricotta Cheesecake

INGREDIENTS

- Ricotta Cheese: 1 cup
- Cream Cheese: 1/2 cup, softened
- Sugar: 1/3 cup
- Eggs: 2 large
- Lemon Zest: 1 tablespoon
- Lemon Juice: 2 tablespoons
- Vanilla Extract: 1/2 teaspoon
- All-Purpose Flour: 2 tablespoons
- Salt: A pinch

Prep Time: 15 min

Cook Time: 50 min

Serves: 4

Nutritional Info (per serving):

Calories: 280/Protein: 10g/Carbs:20g/Fats: 18g/Fiber: 0g/Sodium: 180mg

DIRECTIONS

Preheat Oven: 350°F (175°C). Grease a 6-inch springform pan.
Beat ricotta, cream cheese, and sugar until smooth. Add eggs, lemon zest, juice, vanilla, flour, and salt. Mix well.
Pour into pan, bake for 45-50 min until set. Cool for 1 hour.
Enjoy with fresh berries or a drizzle of honey.

Turkish Pistachio and Rosewater Lokum (Turkish Delight)

INGREDIENTS

- Granulated Sugar: 1 cup
- Water: 1 1/2 cups, divided
- Cornstarch: 1/4 cup
- Lemon Juice: 1 teaspoon
- Rosewater: 1 tablespoon
- Pistachios: 1/4 cup, chopped
- Powdered Sugar: 1/4 cup (for dusting)
- Optional: A few drops of natural food coloring (pink or red)

 Prep Time: 20 min

 Cook Time: 45 min

 Serves: 4

Nutritional Info (per serving):

Calories: 150/Protein: 1g/Carbs: 35g/Fats: 2g/Fiber: 0.5g/Sodium: 10mg

DIRECTIONS

Boil sugar, 1/2 cup water, and lemon juice until syrup reaches 240°F (115°C), about 25-30 min.

Mix cornstarch with 1 cup water and cook until thickened about 5-7 min.

Slowly add syrup to the cornstarch mixture and cook until thick and golden, about 20 min. Stir in rosewater, food coloring, and pistachios.

Pour into a greased 8x8-inch dish, excellent, and set for 4 hours or overnight. Cut into squares and dust with powdered sugar.

French Lavender and Honey Ice Cream

INGREDIENTS

- Heavy Cream: 1 cup
- Whole Milk: 1 cup
- Honey: 1/4 cup
- Dried Culinary Lavender: 1 tablespoon
- Egg Yolks: 3 large
- Vanilla Extract: 1 teaspoon
- Pinch of Salt

 Prep Time: 15 min

 Cook Time: 10 min

 Serves: 4

Nutritional Info (per serving):

Calories: 230/Protein: 4g/Carbs:18g/Fats: 16g/Fiber: 0g/Sodium: 50mg

DIRECTIONS

Simmer cream, milk, and lavender. Remove from heat, steep for 10 min, then strain.

Whisk egg yolks, honey, and salt. Gradually mix in warm cream, then cook over low heat until thickened.

Stir in vanilla, cool, then refrigerate for 2-3 hours.

Pour into an ice cream maker and churn. Freeze for at least 2 hours before serving.

Garnish with honey or fresh lavender if desired.

Spanish Flan with Caramelized Sugar

INGREDIENTS

- Sugar: 1/2 cup (for caramel)
- Whole Milk: 2 cups
- Eggs: 3 large
- Honey: 1/4 cup (can substitute with sugar)
- Vanilla Extract: 1 teaspoon
- Lemon Zest: 1 teaspoon (optional)
- Pinch of Salt

 Prep Time: 15 min Cook Time: 45 min Serves: 4

Nutritional Info (per serving):

Calories: 220/Protein: 6g/Carbs: 33g/Fats: 7g/Fiber: 0g/Sodium: 80mg

DIRECTIONS

Melt sugar in a saucepan until amber. Pour into four ramekins, coating the bottoms.

Warm milk. Whisk eggs, honey, vanilla, lemon zest, and salt. Slowly mix in warm milk.

Pour custard over caramel in ramekins. Place in a water bath and bake at 350°F for 40-45 min until set.

Cool to room temp, then refrigerate for 2 hours. Run a knife around the edge to serve and invert onto a plate.

Moroccan Orange Salad with Cinnamon and Dates

INGREDIENTS

- Oranges: 4 large, peeled, and thinly sliced
- Medjool Dates: 6, pitted and chopped
- Cinnamon: 1 teaspoon
- Honey: 1 tablespoon (optional)
- Orange Blossom Water: 1 teaspoon (optional for extra flavor)
- Fresh Mint Leaves: 2 tablespoons, chopped
- Pistachios or Almonds: 2 tablespoons, chopped (optional)

 Prep Time: 10 min Cook Time: 0 min Serves: 4

Nutritional Info (per serving):

Calories: 120/Protein: 1g/Carbs:28g/Fats: 1g/Fiber: 4g/Sodium: 0mg

DIRECTIONS

Slice oranges and arrange on a platter.

Sprinkle with chopped dates and cinnamon.

Drizzle with honey and orange blossom water if desired.

Top with mint and nuts if using.

Greek Yogurt Parfait with Honey and Figs

INGREDIENTS

- Greek Yogurt: 2 cups (plain, full-fat or low-fat)
- Honey: 4 tablespoons
- Fresh Figs: 8, quartered
- Granola: 1/2 cup (optional)
- Walnuts: 1/4 cup, chopped (optional)
- Cinnamon: 1/2 teaspoon (optional)
- Fresh Mint: For garnish (optional)

Prep Time: 10 min

Cook Time: 0 min

Serves: 4

Nutritional Info (per serving):

Calories: 220/Protein: 8g/Carbs: 30g/Fats: 8g/Fiber: 3g/Sodium: 60mg

DIRECTIONS

Divide the Greek yogurt evenly among four serving glasses or bowls.
Drizzle one tablespoon of honey over each yogurt portion.
Arrange the quartered figs on top of the yogurt and honey.
Sprinkle with granola, chopped walnuts, and a pinch of cinnamon if desired.
Garnish with fresh mint leaves and serve immediately.

Portuguese Custard Tarts (Pastéis de Nata)

INGREDIENTS

- Puff Pastry: 1 sheet (store-bought or homemade)
- Milk: 1/2 cup
- Heavy Cream: 1/2 cup
- Sugar: 1/4 cup
- Egg Yolks: 3 large
- Cornstarch: 1 tablespoon
- Vanilla Extract: 1 teaspoon
- Lemon Zest: 1 teaspoon
- Ground Cinnamon: For dusting

Prep Time: 20 min

Cook Time: 25 min

Serves: 4

Nutritional Info (per serving):

Calories: 220/Protein: 4g/Carbs:20g/Fats: 14g/Fiber: 1g/Sodium: 100mg

DIRECTIONS

Preheat Oven: 400°F (200°C).
Roll out puff pastry, cut into 3-inch circles, and press into a muffin tin.
Heat milk, cream, sugar, and cornstarch until thickened. Remove from heat, whisk in egg yolks, vanilla, and lemon zest.
Pour custard into pastry shells. Bake for 20-25 minutes until golden.
Cool and dust with cinnamon if desired.

Saffron and Cardamom Panna Cotta

INGREDIENTS

- Heavy Cream: 1 cup
- Whole Milk: 1 cup
- Honey: 1/4 cup
- Gelatin: 1 teaspoon (unflavored)
- Saffron: A pinch (about 8-10 strands)
- Ground Cardamom: 1/4 teaspoon
- Vanilla Extract: 1/2 teaspoon
- Water: 2 tablespoons (for blooming gelatin)

 Prep Time: 15 min

 Cook Time: 10 min

 Serves: 4

Nutritional Info (per serving):

Calories: 180/Protein: 3g/Carbs: 15g/Fats: 12g/Fiber: 0g/Sodium: 30mg

DIRECTIONS

Sprinkle gelatin over 2 tbsp of cold water, let sit for 5 min.

Combine cream, milk, honey, saffron, and cardamom in a saucepan. Heat until hot but not boiling. Remove from heat, stir in vanilla.

Stir the bloomed gelatin into the warm cream mixture until fully dissolved.

Pour into 4 cups of ramekins. Refrigerate for 4 hours until set.

Serve chilled and garnish with saffron, cardamom, or fresh fruit.

Italian Tiramisu with Marsala Wine

INGREDIENTS

- Mascarpone Cheese: 1 cup
- Greek Yogurt (plain, full-fat): 1/2 cup (to lighten the dish)
- Egg Yolks: 2 large
- Sugar: 1/4 cup
- Marsala Wine: 2 tablespoons
- Espresso: 1/2 cup, cooled
- Ladyfingers: 12-16 pieces
- Unsweetened Cocoa Powder: 1 tablespoon (for dusting)
- Dark Chocolate Shavings: 1 tablespoon (optional for garnish)

 Prep Time: 20 min

 Cook Time: 0 min

 Serves: 4

Nutritional Info (per serving):

Calories: 350/Protein: 6g/Carbs:35g/Fats: 20g/Fiber: 1g/Sodium: 70mg

DIRECTIONS

Whisk egg yolks and sugar until thick. Add mascarpone, yogurt, and Marsala; mix until smooth.

Briefly dip ladyfingers in espresso.

Layer dipped ladyfingers and cream mixture in a dish or cups.

Refrigerate for 4 hours or overnight.

Dust with cocoa powder and garnish with chocolate shavings if desired.

Spanish Almond Cake (Tarta de Santiago)

INGREDIENTS

- Almond Flour: 1 cup (100g)
- Sugar: 1/2 cup (100g)
- Eggs: 2 large
- Lemon Zest: 1 teaspoon
- Cinnamon: 1/2 teaspoon
- Vanilla Extract: 1/2 teaspoon
- Powdered Sugar: For dusting
- Optional: 1/4 teaspoon almond extract

 Prep Time: 15 min
 Cook Time: 30-35 min
 Serves: 4

Nutritional Info (per serving):

Calories: 250/Protein: 7g/Carbs: 23g/Fats: 14g/Fiber: 3g/Sodium: 30mg

DIRECTIONS

Preheat Oven: 350°F (175°C). Grease and line a 6-inch round cake pan.
Beat eggs and sugar until frothy. Fold in almond flour, lemon zest, cinnamon, vanilla, and optional almond extract.
Pour batter into the pan. Bake for 30-35 minutes until golden and set.
Cool, then dust with powdered sugar.

Sicilian Granita with Fresh Berries

INGREDIENTS

- Water: 2 cups
- Sugar: 1/4 cup
- Fresh Lemon Juice: 1/4 cup
- Fresh Orange Juice: 1/4 cup
- Lemon Zest: 1 teaspoon
- Fresh Berries: 1 cup (mixed berries like strawberries, blueberries, raspberries)
- Fresh Mint Leaves: For garnish (optional)

 Prep Time: 15 min
 Cook Time: 0 min
 Serves: 4

Nutritional Info (per serving):

Calories: 70/Protein: 0g/Carbs:18g/Fats: 0g/Fiber: 1g/Sodium: 5 mg

DIRECTIONS

Heat water and sugar in a saucepan until dissolved. Cool slightly.
Stir in lemon juice, orange juice, and lemon zest.
Pour into a shallow dish and freeze, scraping with a fork every 30 minutes, until fluffy, about 4-5 hours.
Scoop granita into bowls, top with fresh berries, and garnish with mint if desired.

Italian Affogato with Espresso and Amaretto

INGREDIENTS

- Vanilla Gelato or Ice Cream: 4 small scoops (about 1 cup total)
- Freshly Brewed Espresso: 4 shots (about 1/2 cup)
- Amaretto Liqueur: 2 tablespoons (optional)
- Almonds: 1/4 cup, chopped and toasted (optional for garnish)
- Dark Chocolate Shavings: 2 tablespoons (optional for garnish)

 Prep Time: 5 min
 Cook Time: 0 min
 Serves: 4

Nutritional Info (per serving):

Calories: 150/Protein: 3g/Carbs: 15g/Fats: 8g/Fiber: 0g/Sodium: 50mg

DIRECTIONS

Brew 4 shots of fresh espresso.
Place one scoop of vanilla gelato or ice cream into each serving cup.
Pour a shot of hot espresso over the gelato.
Add 1/2 tablespoon of Amaretto liqueur to each cup if using.
Garnish with toasted almonds and dark chocolate shavings if desired.
Serve immediately before the gelato melts completely.

Tunisian Almond and Orange Blossom Water Cookies

INGREDIENTS

- Almond Flour: 1 cup
- Sugar: 1/4 cup
- Egg White: 1 large
- Orange Blossom Water: 1 tablespoon
- Lemon Zest: 1 teaspoon
- Baking Powder: 1/4 teaspoon
- Salt: A pinch
- Sliced Almonds: 1/4 cup (for topping)
- Powdered Sugar: For dusting (optional)

 Prep Time: 15 min
 Cook Time: 15 min
 Serves: 4

Nutritional Info (per serving):

Calories: 120/Protein: 3g/Carbs:10g/Fats: 8g/Fiber: 2g/Sodium: 30 mg

DIRECTIONS

Preheat Oven: 350°F (175°C). Line a baking sheet with parchment paper.
Combine almond flour, sugar, baking powder, and salt. Add egg white, orange blossom water, and lemon zest. Mix until a sticky dough forms.
Roll dough into 1 tbsp balls, flatten slightly, and top with sliced almonds.
Bake for 12-15 minutes until the edges are golden. Cool on a wire rack.Dust with powdered sugar if desired.

Chapter 11
4 Weeks Meal Plan
and Shopping List

Week 1 Shopping List

Produce	Dairy	Meat, Poultry, and Seafood	Pantry Staples	Canned and Jarred Goods
• Spinach: 2 lbs • Fresh Herbs (Dill, Parsley, Mint, Cilantro, Thyme, Basil): 1 bunch each • Lemons: 8 • Quinoa: 1 lb • Cucumbers: 8 • Avocados: 4 large • Kale: 1 large bunch • Beets: 4 medium • Arugula: 1 large bunch • Carrots: 4 medium • Onions: 8 medium • Dried Apricots: 8 oz • Almonds: 1 cup • Orzo: 1 cup • Sundried Tomatoes: 1 cup • Peaches: 4 large • Apples: 4 medium • Barley: 1 cup • Flatbread: 1 pack • Eggplant: 2 medium • Zucchini: 4 medium • Yellow Squash: 2 medium • Tomatoes: 8 large, 2 cups cherry/grape • Bell Peppers: 4 large • Yukon Gold Potatoes: 2 lbs • Garlic: 2 heads • Dates: 1 cup • Bananas: 4 • Mixed Berries: 1 cup	• Feta Cheese: 12 oz • Greek Yogurt: 2 cups • Labneh: 1 cup • Milk/Almond Milk: 1 quart • Cream Cheese: 8 oz • Butter: 1/2 lb • Ricotta Cheese: 8 oz • Parmesan Cheese: 4 oz • Burrata Cheese: 8 oz • Goat Cheese: 8 oz • Eggs: 18 large	• Salmon Fillets: 8 • Tilapia Fillets: 4 • Chicken Thighs: 8 • Cod Fillets: 4 • Smoked Salmon: 8 oz • Mixed Seafood (shrimp, mussels, fish, etc.): 2 lbs • Chorizo: 8 oz	• Olive Oil: 1 bottle • Honey: 1 small jar • Walnuts: 1 cup • Rolled Oats: 2 cups • Orange Blossom Water: 1 tsp • Za'atar Spice Mix: 1/4 cup • Saffron: 1 pinch • Balsamic Glaze: 1 small bottle • Whole Wheat/Sourdough Bread: 1 loaf • Pine Nuts: 1 cup	• Stuffed Grape Leaves (Dolmas): 1 can • Fig Jam: 1 small jar • Capers: 1 small jar • Artichokes (marinated/canned): 1 jar • Olives: 1 cup

Week 1 Meal Plan

	Breakfast	Lunch	Dinner	Snack
Mon day	Mediterranean Frittata with Spinach and Feta	Quinoa Tabbouleh with Fresh Herbs	Grilled Salmon with Dill and Lemon	Greek Yogurt Parfait with Honey and Walnuts
Tues day	Za'atar Seasoned Avocado Toast	Tuscan White Bean and Kale Soup	Baked Cod with Crispy Garlic and Chorizo Crumbs	Stuffed Grape Leaves (Dolmas)
Wedn esday	Pistachio and Orange Blossom Oatmeal	Roasted Beet and Arugula Salad with Goat Cheese	Moroccan Chicken Tagine with Apricots and Almonds	Mediterranean Cheese Platter with Fig Jam
Thurs day	Warm Barley and Apple Breakfast Bowl	Spinach and Orzo Salad with Sundried Tomatoes	Herb-crusted Tilapia with Lemon Butter	Lemon and Thyme Marinated Artichokes
Fri day	Cucumber and Herb Labneh on Toast	Grilled Peach and Burrata Salad with Balsamic Glaze	Mediterranean Baked Salmon with Feta and Spinach	Baba Ganoush with Warm Flatbread
Satur day	Mediterranean Morning Smoothie with Dates and Almonds	Classic Gazpacho with Fresh Tomatoes and Cucumber	Saffron-Infused Seafood Stew	Crispy Polenta Bites with Olive Tapenade
Sun day	Smoked Salmon and Cream Cheese Crepes	Mediterranean Roasted Vegetable Medley with Herbs de Provence	Greek Lemon Chicken with Potatoes	Caprese Skewers with Balsamic Reduction

Week 2 Shopping List

Produce	Dairy	Meat, Poultry, and Seafood	Pantry Staples	Canned and Jarred Goods
• Spinach: 3 lbs • Garlic: 2 heads • Lemons: 8 • Bell Peppers: 8 large, 6 red • Prunes: 1 cup • Onions: 6 medium • Asparagus: 2 bunches • Tomatoes: 8 large, 2 cups cherry • Fava Beans: 1 cup (fresh or canned) • Mint, Basil, Oregano: 1 bunch each • Pears: 4 medium • Pecans: 1/2 cup • Melon: 1 large • Eggs: 18 large • Barley: 1 cup • Mixed Vegetables: 4 cups • Citrus Fruits: 4 (oranges, grapefruit, lemon) • Cucumber: 2 medium	• Ricotta Cheese: 16 oz • Feta Cheese: 8 oz • Greek Yogurt: 2 cups • Butter: 1/2 lb • Parmesan Cheese: 4 oz • Milk/Almond Milk: 1 quart	• Chicken Thighs: 8 • Lamb (Stewing Cuts): 1.5 lbs • Sea Bass Fillets: 4 • Prosciutto: 8 slices • Swordfish Steaks: 4 • Octopus: 1.5 lbs	• Olive Oil: 1 bottle • Honey: 1 small jar • Walnuts: 1 cup • Almonds: 1 cup • Figs (Dried): 1 cup • Lentils: 1 cup • Quinoa: 1 cup • Risotto Rice: 1.5 cups • Whole Wheat/Sourdough Bread: 1 loaf • Pine Nuts: 1/2 cup • Farfalle Pasta: 1 lb • Capers: 1/4 cup	• Artichoke Hearts: 1 jar • Roasted Red Peppers: 1 jar • Olives: 1 jar • Marinated Olives: 1 jar • Tomato Sauce: 2 cups • Pistachios: 1/2 cup • Almond Flour: 1 cup • Balsamic Vinegar: 1 small bottle

Week 2 Meal Plan

	Breakfast	Lunch	Dinner	Snack
Mon day	Spinach and Ricotta Breakfast Pitas	Lentil and Spinach Soup with Lemon	Chicken Marbella with Olives and Prunes	Baked Pear with Honey and Pecans
Tues day	Almond and Fig Breakfast Bars	Quinoa Stuffed Bell Peppers	Moroccan Lamb Tagine with Prunes and Almonds	Whipped Feta with Honey and Pistachios
Wedn esday	Poached Eggs over Garlic Spinach and Toast	Lemon Basil Risotto with Asparagus	Mediterranean Sea Bass with Olives and Tomatoes	Fava Bean and Mint Crostini
Thurs day	Artichoke and Roasted Pepper Omelet	Roasted Red Pepper and Almond Soup	Italian Chicken Cacciatore with Olives and Tomatoes	Prosciutto-wrapped melon with Basil
Fri day	Greek Yogurt Parfait with Honey and Walnuts	Warm Barley and Roasted Vegetable Salad	Grilled Octopus with Oregano and Lemon	Spinach and Feta Phyllo Triangles (Spanakopita Bites)
Satur day	Mediterranean Egg White Scramble	Pesto Pasta Salad with Pine Nuts and Cherry Tomatoes	Swordfish Steaks with Capers and Roasted Peppers	Marinated Olives with Citrus and Herbs
Sun day	Citrus and Mint Fruit Salad with Greek Yogurt	Farfalle with Spinach and Ricotta	Chicken Souvlaki with Cucumber-Yogurt Sauce	Spicy Muhammara (Red Pepper and Walnut Spread)

Week 3 Shopping List

Produce	Dairy	Meat, Poultry, and Seafood	Pantry Staples	Canned and Jarred Goods
• Olives: 1 jar • Sundried Tomatoes: 1 jar • Onions: 8 medium • Fennel Bulbs: 2 • Eggplant: 4 medium • Tomatoes: 8 large • Spinach: 2 lbs • Watermelon: 1 small • Cucumbers: 4 medium • Mushrooms: 2 cups • Garlic: 2 heads • Basil, Dill, Mint, Parsley: 1 bunch each • Oranges: 4 • Lemons: 6 • Artichoke Hearts: 1 jar • Carrots: 4 medium • Avocados: 4 large • Farro: 1 cup • Preserved Lemons: 1 jar	• Feta Cheese: 12 oz • Butter: 1/2 lb • Eggs: 18 large • Ricotta Cheese: 8 oz • Cream Cheese: 8 oz • Parmesan Cheese: 4 oz • Milk/Almond Milk: 1 quart	• Chicken Breasts: 4 • Tuna Steaks: 4 • Chicken Thighs: 8 • Rack of Lamb: 1 • Smoked Salmon: 8 oz • Pork Chops: 4 • Fish (for Tagine): 1.5 lbs • Beef Osso Bucco: 4 cuts	• Olive Oil: 1 bottle • Balsamic Vinegar: 1 small bottle • Honey: 1 small jar • Pine Nuts: 1/2 cup • Flour: 2 cups • Panko Breadcrumbs: 1 cup • Za'atar Spice Mix: 1/4 cup • Quinoa: 1 cup • Chia Seeds: 1/4 cup • Dried Apricots: 1 cup • Pimentón (Smoked Paprika): 1 small jar	• Roasted Red Peppers: 1 jar • Capers: 1 jar • Pistachios: 1/2 cup • Anchovies: 1 small jar • Tomato Sauce: 2 cups

Week 3 Meal Plan

	Breakfast	Lunch	Dinner	Snack
Mon day	Savory Muffin with Olives and Sundried Tomatoes	Caramelized Onion and Fennel Soup	Balsamic Glazed Chicken with Vegetables	Eggplant and Tomato Bruschetta
Tues day	Baked Eggs with Spinach and Tomato Sauce	Watermelon, Cucumber, and Feta Salad	Seared Tuna Steaks with Olive Tapenade	Baba Ganoush with Warm Flatbread
Wedn esday	Olive and Tomato Breakfast Bruschetta	Creamy Tomato Basil Soup with Roasted Garlic	Mediterranean Herb-Crusted Rack of Lamb	Seafood Stuffed Mushrooms
Thurs day	Feta and Dill Breakfast Scones	Shaved Fennel and Orange Salad with Olives and Dill	Chicken Piccata with Capers and Lemon Butter Sauce	Smoked Salmon and Cream Cheese Cucumber Bites
Fri day	Quinoa and Chia Porridge with Apricots	Artichoke and Olive Orzo Salad	Spanish Pork Chops with Pimentón and Garlic	Caponata: Sicilian Eggplant Stew with Capers and Vinegar
Satur day	Za'atar Seasoned Avocado Toast	Creamy Farro Risotto with Mushrooms and Spinach	Fish Tagine with Preserved Lemon and Olives	Garlic and Herb Baked Feta
Sun day	Mediterranean Frittata with Spinach and Feta	Moroccan Spiced Carrot Salad with Orange and Mint	Italian Beef Osso Bucco with Gremolata	Greek Fava with Caramelized Onions and Capers

Week 4 Shopping List

Produce	Dairy	Meat, Poultry, and Seafood	Pantry Staples	Canned and Jarred Goods
• Pistachios: 1/2 cup • Orange blossom water: 1 tbsp • Saffron threads: 1/4 tsp • Red bell pepper: 1 • Onion: 3 • Garlic: 8 cloves • Artichokes: 8 small • Lemon: 3 • Fresh thyme: 1 bunch • Barley: 1 cup • Apples: 2 • Spinach: 10 oz (4 cups) • Sundried tomatoes: 1/2 cup • Butternut squash: 1 small • Fresh sage: 2 tbsp • Eggplant: 1 large • Dates: 1/2 cup • Fennel: 1 bulb • Fresh herbs (parsley, mint, dill): 1 bunch each • Cucumber: 1 large • Asparagus: 1 bunch • Mint: 1 bunch	• Milk: 2 cups • Cream cheese: 1/2 cup • Yogurt: 1 cup • Labneh: 1/2 cup • Feta cheese: 1 cup • Goat cheese: 1/2 cup • Ricotta cheese: 1/2 cup	• Beef stew meat: 1 lb • Veal: 1 lb • Chicken breast: 1 lb • Pork roast: 1 lb • Calamari: 1 lb • Smoked Salmon: 8 oz • Sardines: 4-6 fillets • Mussels: 1 lb • Mixed seafood: 1 lb (shrimp, mussels, clams)	• Rolled oats: 1 cup • Farro: 1 cup • Orzo: 1 cup • Quinoa: 1 cup • Whole wheat flour: 1/2 cup • Honey: 1/4 cup • Olive oil: 1/2 cup • Vinegar (balsamic, white wine): 1/4 cup each • Garlic powder, Onion powder, Red pepper flakes, Ground cumin, Ground coriander: 1 tsp each • Ground cinnamon: 1/2 tsp • Tomato paste: 2 tbsp	• Sun-dried tomatoes: 1/2 cup • Olives: 1/2 cup • Capers: 2 tbsp • Artichokes: 1 cup (jarred) • Roasted red peppers: 1 cup (jarred) • Fig jam: 1/2 cup

Week 4 Meal Plan

	Breakfast	Lunch	Dinner	Snack
Monday	Pistachio and Orange Blossom Oatmeal	Saffron-Infused Paella with Mixed Seafood	Provençal Beef Stew with Red Wine and Olives	Lemon and Thyme Marinated Artichokes
Tuesday	Warm Barley and Apple Breakfast Bowl	Spinach and Orzo Salad with Sundried Tomatoes	Spicy Mussels in Tomato and White Wine Sauce	Roasted Red Peppers Stuffed with Herbed Goat Cheese
Wednesday	Mediterranean Morning Smoothie with Dates and Almonds	Mediterranean Quinoa with Sun-Dried Tomatoes and Feta	Moroccan Spiced Sardines	Grilled Eggplant with Yogurt and Pomegranate Seeds
Thursday	Smoked Salmon and Cream Cheese Crepes	Butternut Squash and Sage Soup	Calamari Stuffed with Rice and Herbs	Mediterranean Cheese Platter with Fig Jam
Friday	Cucumber and Herb Labneh on Toast	Tuscan Farro Salad with Roasted Vegetables	Grilled Veal with Lemon and Herbs	Spinach and Feta Phyllo Triangles (Spanakopita Bites)
Saturday	Spinach and Ricotta Breakfast Pitas	Mediterranean Roasted Vegetable Medley with Herbs de Provence	Chicken and Fig Skewers with Honey-Lemon Glaze	Spicy Muhammara (Red Pepper and Walnut Spread)
Sunday	Poached Eggs over Garlic Spinach and Toast	Grilled Asparagus and Quinoa Salad with Feta and Mint	Tuscan Roast Pork with Fennel and Rosemary	Garlic and Herb Baked Feta

Made in United States
Orlando, FL
09 November 2024